ARCHITECTURE FOR
SCIENCE

ARCHITECTURE FOR
SCIENCE

MICHAEL J. CROSBIE

Published in Australia in 2004 by
The Images Publishing Group Pty Ltd
ABN 89 059 734 431
6 Bastow Place, Mulgrave, Victoria, 3170, Australia
Telephone: +61 3 9561 5544 Facsimile: +61 3 9561 4860
Email: books@images.com.au
Website: www.imagespublishinggroup.com

National Library of Australia
Cataloguing-in-Publication entry:

Crosbie, Michael J.
Architecture for science.

Includes index.
ISBN 1 920744 64 9.

1. Laboratories – United States – Design and construction.
2. Laboratories – United States – Pictorial works. I. Title.

727.5500973

Designed by The Graphic Image Studio Pty Ltd, Mulgrave, Australia
Website: www.tgis.com.au

Film by Mission Productions Limited
Printed by Sing Cheong Printing Co. Ltd. Hong Kong

IMAGES has included on its website a page for special notices in relation to this
and our other publications. Please visit this site: www.imagespublishinggroup.com

CONTENTS

As a building type, laboratories are a relatively recent invention. Architecture specifically designed for scientific investigation has been around just over a century—the life of a mayfly when one considers such building types as libraries, churches, and schools. Laboratories are an invention of our culture—a modern, scientific society—that requires special equipment, space, and accommodation for activities that have grown increasingly specialized and dangerous over the past decades. In fact, laboratories today have all kinds of security issues to address as well. They not only have to keep things inside from getting out, but they also have to ensure that terrorists, saboteurs, and industrial spies do not get in. In some cases, these concerns prevent us from showing plans for projects in this book.

One of the characteristics of this relatively new building type is the dependence on technology. This not only means the inclusion of sophisticated equipment (microscopes, freezers, glass washers, centrifuges) but also technology woven through the building to make scientific work possible. Mechanical equipment drives the form and function of many labs. A startling example is the Contained Research Facility at the University of California, Davis, for agricultural research. This building required Bio-Safety Level 2 and 3 labs, which means that most of its volume is devoted to mechanical equipment. The building's form is derived from the architect's decision to contain all of that hardware in the second story, inside the roof form. This helps to relate the building to its agricultural context, and also keeps its scale low.

Reliance on high-powered mechanical systems and energy makes laboratories tough candidates for sustainable design. This book demonstrates that this is changing. A good example of the new trend toward 'green' lab buildings is the Bocas del Toro Laboratory in Panama. This building—dedicated to education as well as research—is raised above its fragile mangrove swamp site on concrete piers to minimize its impact as it touches down. The building also mitigates the effects of the sun with extensive

PREFACE

MICHAEL J. CROSBIE
ESSEX, CONNECTICUT

shading, while maximizing the use of natural light for less energy consumption. The building is designed to collect and use rainwater, and to recycle wastewater as well. And on its roof is a 38 kW array of photovoltaic cells that help provide for the building's power needs. Another laboratory that accentuates sustainability is the Institute for Forestry and Nature Research in Wageningen, the Netherlands, which blurs the distinction between where the building ends and where nature begins. Greenery invades the interior, providing a soft environment that helps to reduce stress, rejuvenates the staff, and also helps to purify the wastewater, allowing a 'closed loop' system. Yet another lab—the Franklin Wilkins building at King's College in London—is sustainable in its conversion of a century-old warehouse building. Reuse of existing facilities, especially those that were not laboratories to begin with, is a stiff design challenge, but one that preserves materials and the energy embodied in old structures. These and other buildings presented here are encouraging signs that labs can also be green.

Many of the facilities in this volume are located on college and university campuses, serving not only the needs of researcher but also of students. These laboratories must respond not only to the immediate needs of scientific inquiry, but also be good campus neighbors. The Tome Multidisciplinary Science Building on the campus of Dickinson College uses a local limestone on its exterior to tie it to other buildings on campus that date from a century-and-a-half ago. The Science and Technology Research Building at the University of California, Los Angeles helps to define the new edge of a quadrangle and provides shaded space for the students to enjoy the mild climate. This building is essentially a big barn space inside, but outside it responds to the campus context with a sensitive scale and an inventive use of materials.

Another example of sensitive campus planning is the new Science Center at Oberlin College, designed by Payette Associates (who wrote the illuminating Introduction to this book). The design mends past planning mistakes on the campus, reuses some existing structures, and helps to create a new quadrangle to reinforce campus identity and sociability. It also provides a dynamic center for the sciences, which encourages researchers to cross-pollinate disciplines—a key factor in advancement in the sciences. In fact many of the labs represented here have as their goal the provision of informal settings for chance meetings and conversations so that ideas can be shared and connections can be made. Another Payette project, the Maxwell Dworkin Laboratory at Harvard University, has at its heart a large, inviting scissor stair that encourages casual interaction among staff as they move throughout the building. A similar strategy can be seen in the Gnomics and Proteomic Research Building at McGill University, where the stair becomes the primary architectural feature of the interior, and a device for mixing the staff.

In such highly designed environments, where first consideration often seems given to the work at hand rather than the comfort of the staff, it is important to maintain connections to sunlight and views to reconnect people to the outside world and to reduce the stress associated with intensive research. Many projects in this volume accent the use of natural light as a building amenity. This is often achieved with central atria that fill the building with the sun. For example, the Donald Danforth Plant Science Center outside of St. Louis, Missouri, has at its heart an atrium that brings in soft, northern light and also allows for open circulation via two dramatic staircases, which enliven this space throughout the day. At the Harvey W. Wiley Federal Building in College Park, Maryland, the central atrium becomes the library, encouraging staff to also use it as a workspace. Other labs use borrowed light from offices at the building's outer edge to bring natural illumination deep inside the central lab spaces. These techniques remind us that although this fairly new building type is a product of science, it still must respond to the deepest and most ancient needs of those inside who need light, air, and social interaction to produce their best work.

The rapid change in science and its methodologies are exciting, invigorating challenges for architects. We are fascinated by the multi-layered aspects of contemporary human inquiry. We become part of the commitment to make places that support and enable scientific advancement and learning to improve the human condition. We strive for our creative process to result in a place of creative discovery.

Designers who work on successful buildings for science approach this building type from several points of view. As architects, we believe beautiful and humanistic surroundings inspire creativity and intellectual achievement. As laboratory planners, we strive for ideas that define new and innovative ways for people to work collaboratively, efficiently, and safely in a highly technical environment. As campus planners, we are thoughtful in how we place a new building on a campus because we respect the character of its past and its future.

THE HIGH COST OF RESEARCH

Buildings for science today are more sophisticated than yesterday's utilitarian and functional 'research laboratories.' This is prompted by several trends. First, scientific investigation has produced remarkable advances in all areas of science and has resulted in increased funding. Second, new instruments, utilities, chemicals, and gases require specialized environments and infrastructure. Third, there is an expanding need for shared core facilities such as analytical instrumentation and animals. Finally, research programs have become multidisciplinary to benefit from the combined knowledge of a broad range of specialists.

A consequence of these trends is high cost. Science buildings are a major financial commitment and owners need to realize a return on investment. Academic institutions try to ensure continuous grant funding and donor contributions by recruiting top-notch scientists for their faculty, while enticing the brightest students who can

INTRODUCTION: ARCHITECTURE FOR SCIENCE

BY PAYETTE ASSOCIATES

pay increased tuition. In turn, the top-notch scientists and the brightest students have their own expectations for pleasant work and living environments. Academic administrations need to balance costs versus benefits because they are accountable to regents or trustees who have become guardians in terms of financial viability, campus planning, and building design.

Corporations have similar goals to recruit top-notch scientists and the brightest employees. These are often the same people being recruited by academia, so there is intense competition. Corporate administrations need to balance costs versus benefits because they are accountable to directors, shareholders, municipalities, and government agencies. Government agencies are accountable to elected officials and ultimately to their constituents.

A new phenomenon is gaining momentum – the research park – where universities, corporations, and governments become partners on a variety of research projects by bringing together talent and resources. This partnering redefines the line between 'open and free' and 'applied' research in terms of intellectual property, copyrights, and profitability.

THE ROLE OF THE CLIENT

Today, science buildings are the symbols of scientific achievement much like high-rise office buildings are symbols of business and commerce. The notion of a laboratory achieving architectural significance was first realized in 1965 with Louis Kahn's Salk Institute in La Jolla, California. This building is well conceived in meeting the needs of function and utility, but goes further, transcending to a poetic spirit and a sense of place.

But why is the Salk Institute able to make this transition to architecture: what makes a successful building for science? Kahn was able to achieve his remarkable design because Jonas Salk was able to clearly articulate his vision for the Institute. There is no substitute for an engaged, well-

informed client. The better the communication between the owner and the design team, the better the result. That said, the nature of the client has become more complicated. Who is the owner? In addition to the 'visionary' (*a la* Salk), the client can comprise several committees with representatives who are designated advocates for researchers, administration, building operations and maintenance, engineering, security, and Environmental Health and Safety (EH&S). These representatives need to be able to communicate the issues to their constituencies and be empowered to make decisions on their behalf. It has been our experience that achieving consensus is more realistic than obtaining 100 percent agreement.

THE NATURE OF RESEARCH

To answer the question of what makes a successful science building, one needs to understand the basic categories of a program for research spaces. These are laboratories, laboratory support (instruments and equipment), offices, core facilities (glasswashing, imaging, and animals), and meeting spaces. For teaching, this also includes classrooms, and common space. The size and relative proportion of these categories varies with the type of science. For example, the needs for biological sciences are different from those of physical sciences. Regardless, each science building has these essential categories. Key to a successful building is the designer's knowledge of how the components of each category are designed and how they are assembled to best meet the needs of owner and users.

As science has become more interdisciplinary, with teams of specialists brought together to solve a common problem, space needs have changed. This has had implications for the lab planner and designer from several aspects. Teams can vary in size, and are rarely the same size over time. The nature of specialists can vary from less intensive needs (such as biology) to more intensive needs (such as organic chemistry). One measure of success is how a building can adapt to changes in use, occupants, and technology over time and within reasonable initial budget constraints.

Another measure of success is whether or not a new building is able to enhance or redefine the culture of the user through spatial arrangement. How do people want to work together? How does a series of interconnected spaces promote interaction that can lead to good science? Is there a perfect design that can be copied? (The answer to the last question is no—every building has its unique requirements in terms of program, people, and context.) However, it has been our experience there is one decision that consistently has the greatest impact on redefining culture: the relationship between Principal Investigator offices and their laboratories.

There are many different ways Principal Investigator (PI) offices can be situated. For example, they can be clustered together to promote communication among the team leaders, which is beneficial when specialists want to collaborate and integrate their collective expertise. It promotes 'open' environments where laboratories are interconnected to accommodate large teams and a sharing of resources. While issues of security between assigned spaces and possible contamination between different types of research are often cited as disadvantages of this approach, it has been our experience that administrators and users prefer this model.

On the other hand, PI offices can be located adjacent to their laboratories where the investigators have hands-on involvement with their research. This approach is gradually losing favor because it promotes isolation, applies to small team sizes, and reduces flexibility to reassign space.

A key driver in science buildings is the net-to-gross square footage ratio, expressed as a percentage and defining the building's efficiency. Owners strive to achieve maximum efficiency because it results in more square footage they can assign to research, thus maximizing their return on investment. The range for a new building may be 55 to 60 percent and for renovations 50 to 55 percent, depending on the building's prior use.

Maximum efficiency has a direct impact on the culture of how the building is used. For example, a layout with a single corridor is more efficient than one with two corridors. A single corridor will tend to have large 'open' laboratories whereas smaller laboratories need two corridors for accessibility.

Another important factor that affects efficiency relates to mechanical systems. If the building can 'plug into' existing campus-wide or public utility systems, the efficiency will be higher. On the other hand, if the building needs to provide its own boilers for steam, chillers for cooling, and generators for emergency power, the efficiency is significantly reduced.

Related to efficiency, there has been a steady increase in the ratio of support space to laboratory space. In biology-related research, what used to be 1:3 is now 1:1 (this does not apply to chemistry or engineering). Support spaces require more flexibility than laboratories because they accommodate special (and changing) requirements of many researchers. The ideal design is for this area to be as open as possible, unencumbered by shafts, closets, and other obstructions.

A responsibility of the design team is to identify alternatives with their related impact on building use and cost. This information provides the basis of discussions with administration and user committees, and facilitates a clear understanding of priorities as the building design progresses.

Mechanical systems can be up to 50 percent of the construction cost of a science building. It is critical for an owner to be a fully informed, active participant in establishing engineering standards and selecting systems that are compatible with the budget and with their capability to maintain and operate the building.

LABORATORIES NEVER AT REST

Why do science buildings need to accommodate change? If the average duration of its research programs is three years, it is conceivable that up to 30 percent of the building can be undergoing some level of intervention at any time. Intervention may be required due to changes in research funding, changes in technology, recruiting, promotions, mergers, acquisitions, legislation, etc. A particular basic science research facility completed within the past two years has experienced changes to 29 percent of the net square feet during construction (before it opened its doors!).

Generally, there are three levels of intervention in terms of the cost of the changes: cosmetic changes within existing rooms (such as repainting, new carpeting); upgrades within existing rooms (such as new utilities, lighting, ceilings, carpeting); and renovation where walls are relocated (all trades are affected). In addition to construction costs related to the intervention, other costs may be incurred for things such as 'down time' when the space is not in use, relocation, assuring ongoing operations in adjacent areas, and code upgrades. Owner project management costs are often higher (by 5 percent), as are contingencies (by 5 to 10 percent) and professional fees (by 25 to 50 percent).

A building designed with flexibility to accommodate change will minimize intervention costs but it will also incur higher first costs. A key objective is to incorporate the most amount of flexibility within budget constraints and in the context of other priorities. Depending on the nature of the project, it has been our experience that the following menu of choices can provide cost effective results:

- *Select a building layout that accommodates reassignment of space.*

- *Consolidate uses that require special needs to the infrastructure.*

- *Broaden application of design criteria to highest appropriate use.*

- *Selectively build-in a 'robust' infrastructure.*

- *Provide a mechanical distribution that accommodates change.*

- *Provide a modular distribution of utilities with valves to isolate zones.*

- *Provide repetitive, modular design.*

- *Select a cost-effective casework system.*

- *Consider use of interstitial space.*

The emphasis on interdisciplinary research has prompted social environments to be an integral part of a science building. Creative ideas come from discussions that can occur spontaneously during a casual encounter, informally during a break, or formally during a meeting or classroom session. In academic settings, communication among and between faculty, students, staff, and administration is essential to the education and mentoring process. In corporate settings, communication between researchers, administration, and marketing is essential to staying in business.

Highly successful science buildings elevate this to a strategic level. What might appear mundane are actually well-placed, well-conceived spaces that enhance opportunities for people to meet, pause, and talk. For example, prime locations could be at mailboxes, at the end of corridors, next to a cluster of offices, or at lab entrances. These may be 'soft spaces,' intimate in scale, with lounge seating, warm colors and natural materials, day lighting, or pleasant views. The spaces may be layered with tools to facilitate productivity, such as computers, marker boards, and audio-visual equipment. This may be 'social engineering' but if a stimulating environment leads to scientific achievement, it is vital to maximize use of social space.

Lately, world-renowned architects have received major commissions to design science buildings even if they are not experienced in this field. Why would an owner select a 'signature' or 'star' architect who is not familiar with the building type to design a very expensive laboratory? The owner may need recognition through the architect's image and identity. It may be the requirement of a donor. Or the owner may be searching for a new prototype, perhaps because the science is new.

Whatever the reason, the 'signature' architect often seeks the advice of a laboratory specialist to collaborate on program and functional aspects of the design. When this collaboration is successful, it advances architecture, technology, education, human interaction, and science. Otherwise, the signature architect is relegated to designing an exterior skin disengaged from the interior's functional program.

THE ROLE OF SECURITY AND SAFETY

Over the years, there has been an increasing concern about security in science buildings. Basic issues relate to personal safety, physical property, intellectual property, and the events of 9/11 have introduced concerns of terrorism. To address these issues, local enforcement agencies or campus police, security consultants, and EH&S have become key participants in the planning process to critique emerging designs and offer recommendations for improvement.

Personal safety is a concern for several reasons. First, some areas of research are controversial and can be the focus of demonstrations by activist groups (stem-cell research and use of animals are good examples). Second, research is a 24-hour activity and it is common for people to be working at off-hours.

For general security, the goal is to limit the number of people in the building during the day and restrict the number of people entering after normal working hours. This can be accomplished by using card readers at entrances, doors, stairways, and elevators. General security involves minimizing places where people can hide, making people feel conspicuous (such as generous amounts of glass), and clear signage to make people aware of their location.

To combat terrorism, common sense suggests restricting unauthorized vehicle access near the building (especially at entrances and loading docks), providing security at the reception area with turnstiles that prevent 'piggybacking' and stop someone with malicious intent from slipping through, and locating air intake louvers where they are not easily accessible.

The project team needs to determine the appropriate level of security in the context of the type of research, location, and the type of security already in place. From a designer's point of view, it is preferable to integrate security requirements into the design to minimize their presence while achieving a pleasant, humanistic work environment. For example, safety experts recently cited a new building for science at Yale University as one of the best laboratories they had assessed, thanks to liberal amounts of interior glass for high visibility and transparency between spaces. A spill or accident will be immediately noticed and corrected.

ENERGY CONSERVATION AND SUSTAINABLE DESIGN

The movement towards more efficient and environmentally sensitive architecture has grown in recent years. In part, this is ethical and responsible, but it is also prompted by the goal to minimize operating costs by conserving energy.

Clients often ask: what is the impact on cost and the schedule if we pursue sustainable design? The best way to answer this question is to have an interactive work session where goals and objectives can be discussed with possible approaches, initial costs, and life-cycle savings. The U.S. Green Building Council administers a rating system, Leadership in Energy and Environmental Design (LEED), that can be used as a guideline or (with the commitment to document and monitor the process) can result in official LEED certification. Whether certified or not, sustainable design is good design. Energy providers can be partners in the design process and may give rebates when energy efficient systems are selected.

For example, consider alternative fume hoods. Fume hoods have the largest demand for air volume, usually conditioned fresh air (passing through the building only once). If 'low flow' fume hoods can be used, they require less air and, consequently, less energy. If air volumes can be reduced, triple glazing on exterior windows then becomes economically feasible, particularly in cold climates.

Heat recovery systems have the potential to reduce a science building's overall energy consumption significantly, given the high air volumes. In particular, heat wheels have been used effectively on an increasing number of laboratories to provide a highly efficient energy transfer mechanism between supply and exhaust streams.

Large exterior windows maximize use of natural light and reduce dependency on artificial light when combined with efficient light controls for perimeter fixtures. Natural light has a positive impact on the quality of interior environments because it is fundamental to our well-being. People feel better when they can look outdoors, relate to the weather, time of day, and time of year. This is especially important in a high-technology lab building where much of the design is based on a clean environment with sensitive instruments and durable finishes.

Coincidentally, large exterior windows are compatible with lab buildings because they have tall floor-to-floor heights and high ceilings to accommodate intensive mechanical and electrical systems. Air conditioning has made buildings wider and to compensate, interior glass in doors and walls brings natural light deeper into spaces.

Other common sustainable choices include green roofs, use of gray water for restroom fixtures and landscape irrigation, and use of local materials.

CONCLUSION

In the coming years, the need to accommodate change will remain. The shift from traditional bench-based laboratories to technology-based spaces is likely to continue. For academic institutions, the government, and corporations looking to retrofit older facilities, this will require creative thinking and planning. For example, additions may meet high-technology requirements while the existing structure is downgraded for less intensive uses.

Collaboration will expand to scientists located at remote sites, promoting the further use of computer technologies for data exchange and teleconferencing for team communications. Increased collaboration among academic, corporations, and government will require security to be an integral part of operations and design.

In academic settings, multimodal teaching (talk, watch, write, listen) will expand the use of computer technologies, as will programs related to distance learning, continuing education, and virtual teaching programs.

Medical research will further develop translational medicine, where clinical research and application is integral with basic research, reinforcing the collaboration between clinicians, Principal Investigators, and pharmaceutical companies. Inpatients and outpatients will become commonplace in the laboratory setting with a corresponding impact on building use and occupancy.

Due to high cost and the time it takes to deliver a science building, new projects will incorporate core facilities to serve the research community beyond the building occupants, thus becoming larger and more expensive.

As we can see, there are many influences on laboratory design. These facilities must be designed for intentional and ad hoc interaction. They must support team-based and individual research in a variety of forms. They must accommodate multiple types of scientific work, including multidisciplinary research that can be either 'open' or highly controlled. They must allow for spatial flexibility over time, and be designed to foster the integrated use of highly sophisticated technology. Laboratory spaces must also include office facilities and presentation spaces associated with fund-raising and business needs. Increasingly, the architects represented in this book are designing science buildings to operate more efficiently and effectively over time. But in all cases, the desire to inspire the lives of the occupants is what motivates architects for science.

Payette Associates, based in Boston, Massachusetts, is a leading architecture firm in the design of laboratories and science facilities.

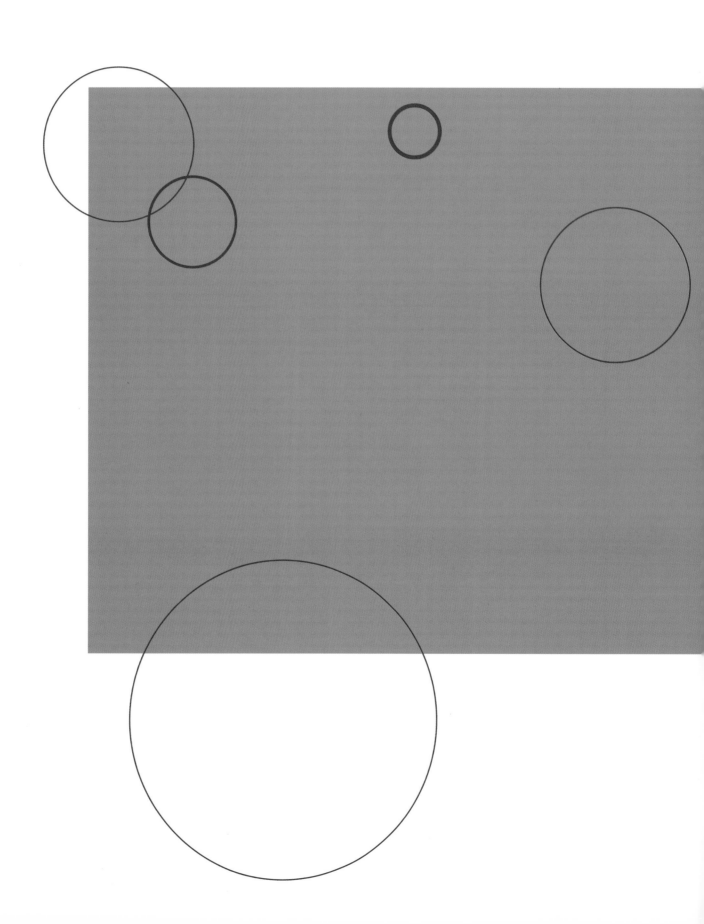

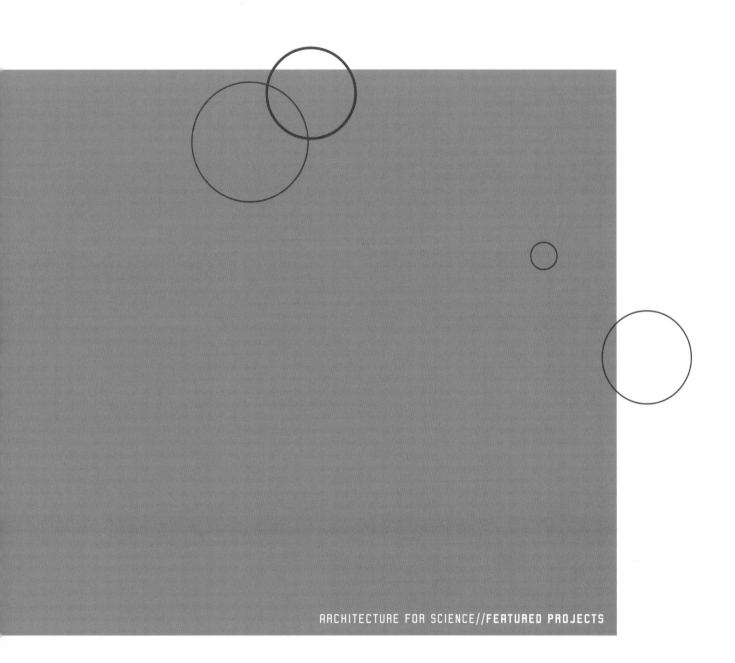

ARCHITECTURE FOR SCIENCE//FEATURED PROJECTS

1

2

The 180,000-square-foot International Vaccine Institute at Seoul National University in Seoul, Korea, was awarded through an international design competition. The complex is carefully sited to create strong ties with the mountainous landscape, while reinforcing a site axis through the complex to Kwanak Mountain. The building form is fractured along an existing footpath that extends through the site to a temple on top of the mountain. Clear functional divisions separate the administration, research, and production areas, all expressed in the building's architectural forms. Terraced gardens and a plaza link them together, much in the tradition of Korean landscape design.

The massing is articulated as three layers and volumes that can be read as one building or several. An intricate system of site walls, terraces, and gardens links the forms together, cradling the mountainous landscape.

Generous public spaces enhance the scientific culture of the institute. Horizontal and vertical openness foster a communal spirit centered on the atrium and also provide natural light to labs and offices. All research labs are oriented toward the mountains and nature, while all the exterior offices face the city. Highly public areas such as the conference center and library are entered from the ground floor, while highly restricted research areas float above the main floor. These two distinct areas are visually connected yet secure, by a communicating stair suspended above the lobby. The large conference rooms cantilevered off the east end of the building face the university.

The T-shaped atrium and lobby spaces are bi-directional, oriented both east–west and north–south, linked with a dramatic sloping skylight over the entire expanse and visually connected to the landscape across both axes.

Exterior fenestration is composed of two systems: glass and granite. The indigenous granite is quarried locally to give the building the natural color of the stone found on the nearby mountains. Stone is used to reflect the planar qualities of the building's faceted massing and is carved with articulated detail at the intersections of the elements.

1   Protected courtyard offers researchers an oasis
2   Viewed from the west, the building emerges like a rock outcropping

INTERNATIONAL VACCINE INSTITUTE

SEOUL NATIONAL UNIVERSITY

PAYETTE ASSOCIATES

3   Detail of southwest façade, with its large expanse of glass wall
4   View of the entry, which the building bends to frame
5   Building negotiates its hilly terrain with stairs and ramps

6

1 Conference center
2 Administration
3 Pilot plant
4 Terrace garden
5 Loading dock (below)
6 Library
7 Research lab

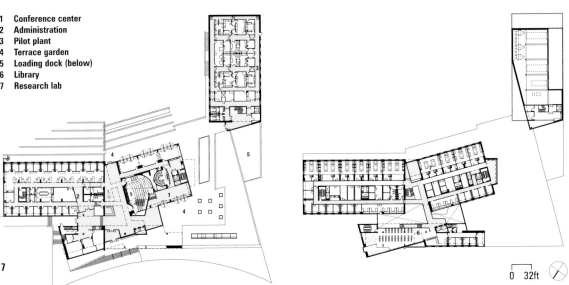

7

0   32ft

6   Entry lobby is found at heart of building

7   Floor plans

8   Lobby area reaches up to skylit roof

Photography: Seung Hoon Yum

8

1 Lab is designed to fit within its wooded setting

2 Exterior of lab is appropriately domestic in scale

2

This laboratory provides offices and support space for the research of computational neuroscience. Rather than traditional bench laboratories, here biologists work on computers.

Located on the campus of Cold Spring Harbor Laboratory in Cold Spring Harbor, New York, the Freeman Laboratory replaced two wood cabins that dated from the early 20th century. These cabins had provided housing in the early days of the laboratory and were much loved for their historic significance. The new building creates a new presence, while reflecting a memory of the laboratory's early days.

The building bends to the contour of a steep hill, wraps around a large oak tree, and helps enclose a new enclave of campus buildings. The building moderates in scale, color, materials, and details between a large neuroscience complex (completed in 1991), a shingled cottage (completed in 1960), and a new laboratory (completed in 1999).

To be easily adaptable, the interiors of the building are kept very simple, working with the vernacular architecture of the Cold Spring Harbor campus. The focus is on providing beautiful views and light throughout. The exterior uses stained concrete and wood siding in random widths to recall the novelty siding of the original cabins. The detailing mimics the random patterns of DNA as they are illustrated in electrophoresis gels. The new porch (a modern version of the porch on the adjacent cottage) and the cornices are detailed like layers of skin that peel back into the building. The roof is made of copper foil shingles.

SAMUEL FREEMAN COMPUTATIONAL NEUROSCIENCE LABORATORY

COLD SPRING HARBOR LABORATORY

CENTERBROOK ARCHITECTS

23

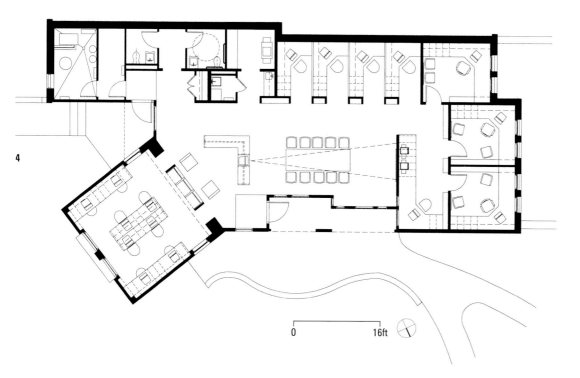

4

3 Lab space receives light from clerestories above

4 Floor plan

5 View from adjacent building of lab's main entrance

6 Wood siding and clerestories help to create a welcoming façade

Photography: Jeff Goldberg/Esto

6

5

1 Building's linear design expresses its classic laboratory floor layout

2 Detail of edge of curtainwall on building's narrow end

3 Detail of masonry façade patterning

Photography: Tom Bonner Photography

1

2

3

The Gonda (Goldschmied) Neuroscience and Genetics Research Center, located on the Los Angeles campus of the University of California, completes the urban plaza at the Westwood Boulevard entrance to the university, and responds to the university's mandate to give primacy to the neurosciences as the home of the Brain Research Institute and the Department of Human Genetics.

The seven-story facility provides a setting for research focusing on the isolation of genetic defects that lead to neurological and other diseases, and the development of interventions to treat and prevent them. Among its core laboratories is the Carol Moss Spivak Microscope Center (a collaboration of UCLA, Lecia Microsystems, and McBain Instruments) that has the capability of imaging individual living cells as they work. Another core lab is dedicated to identifying disease genes through genotyping and sequencing. A bioformation and statistic core will provide researchers with software and mathematics for analysis and interpretation of data. The center also houses a vivarium to support the research programs.

Gonda is connected to the MacDonald Research Center physically and architecturally. The red, masonry walls with a complex ornamentation of tile, brick, and terracotta are referential, relating the buildings closely to each other. Both structures refer subtly to the architectural vocabulary of the UCLA campus. An intimate outdoor plaza separates the Gonda Center from its companion, but the buildings touch by means of a walkway along the south side, and share a common level for services and operations.

While most of the building exterior is patterned masonry, a faceted, glass curtain wall on the south façade expresses naturally lit interior spaces that are dedicated to incidental interaction and communication between researchers. The prototypical plan has offices and labs designed for maximum flexibility and services 33 core research modules with state-of-the-art equipment.

GONDA (GOLDSCHMIED) NEUROSCIENCE AND GENETICS RESEARCH CENTER

LEE, BURKHART, LIU
VENTURI, SCOTT BROWN
AND ASSOCIATES

Harvard University's departments of computer science and electrical engineering required a new and larger facility to consolidate the teaching and research activities of its existing faculty and eight new appointments. Located on the western edge of Harvard's science precinct, in Cambridge, Massachusetts, the new building accommodates the shift from the faculty's theoretical study to experimental and systems work.

The building includes nearly 100,000 square feet of new academic space on an extremely constrained site. Since a high-rise structure was not possible, the resulting floor plates extend nearly to the edges of the available building area.

In order to mitigate the structure's mass, the design solution divides the building into manageable parts that respond to two distinct site conditions and articulate the spatial organization. A brick exterior wall wraps the building to the north and complements the traditional structures on the adjacent Law School quad. Facing the street edge, a lighter, more transparent façade of glass curtainwall and aluminum sunscreens celebrates the role of technology and discovery within the new building. The design also extends the boundary of the engineering precinct to the north while reinforcing the continuity between campus spaces to the east and west.

The ground-floor classrooms are connected by a linear lobby on the south side of the building. The upper floors—containing labs interspersed with offices for faculty, post-doctoral researchers, and graduate students—are linked by an open and translucent stairway at the building's center.

The translucent scissor stair, combined with generous open lounges, promotes social interaction between disciplines and increases the opportunities for serendipitous exchanges—a crucial part of the scientific research and learning process.

Opposite:
Scissor stair at heart of building promotes informal interaction

MAXWELL DWORKIN LABORATORY

HARVARD UNIVERSITY

PAYETTE ASSOCIATES

2

3

2 From the east, the laboratory reaches out with a knife-edge wall

3 Building from the west, as it faces the law school quad

4 Floor plan

5 Detail of the east end of building

1 Lobby
2 Seminar room
3 Distance learning seminar room
4 Break room
5 Student lounge
6 Office

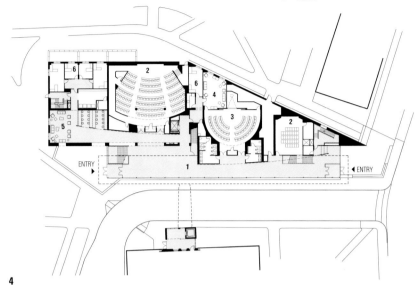

4

5

31

Opposite:
On its south edge, the laboratory connects to Pierce Hall

7   Lounges offer quiet places for study

Photography: Jeff Goldberg/Esto

7

1

2

3

uilding Q is the new cornerstone building for Pharmacia's large-scale research campus in Skokie, Illinois. The crisply detailed exterior's precast panels and fenestration blend with other buildings on campus. The design goal was to provide a safe, adaptable, and competitive workplace to expand Pharmacia's ability to support its pharmaceutical business.

Pharmacia wisely chose to put the majority of the building budget into the labs and other interior elements that the staff would benefit from. For example, each laboratory 'neighborhood' has its own color scheme, with coordinating colors drawn from adjacent lab neighborhoods.

Two atria encourage staff interaction, allow natural light to penetrate throughout the labs and other interior spaces, and have become gathering places for staff from surrounding buildings. Shafts of sunlight penetrating deep within the building, a fountain providing soothing white noise, and a playful palette of colors all contribute to an environment that is professional yet comfortable. Labs surround the atria on both sides, with glass walls for light transfer to the lab interior. Researcher offices are found adjacent the lab, along the building's perimeter. The offices are either open to the labs or separated by glass walls to permit researchers to monitor research activity.

The building's sustainable techniques and materials help save over $800,000 per year in energy costs. Nearly all the materials in the building came from within a 300-mile radius, so they possess less embodied energy. Overall, the facility consumes 40 percent less energy than comparable facilities.

1   Curved form helps to identify the building's front door
2   View of the building's welcoming entrance
3   Bold color is used to distinguish the entrance on the façade

PHARMACIA BUILDING Q

FLAD ASSOCIATES

35

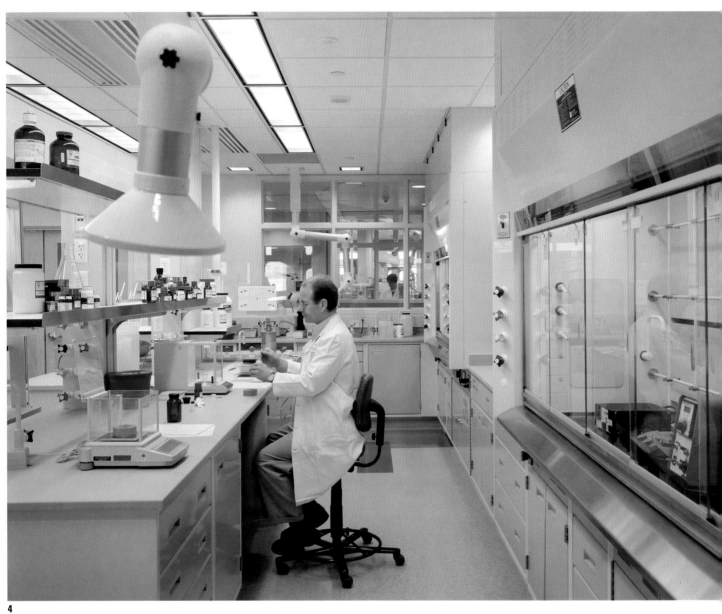

4

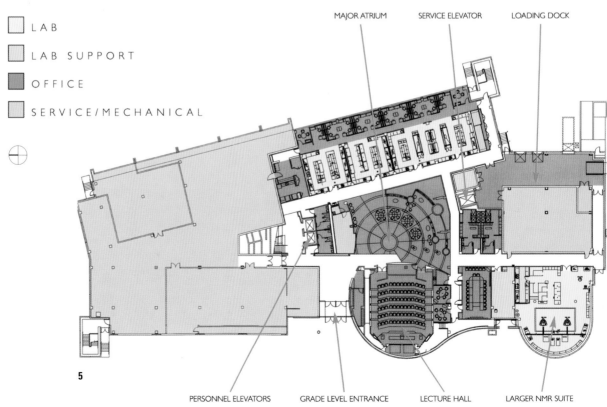

☐ LAB
☐ LAB SUPPORT
☐ OFFICE
☐ SERVICE/MECHANICAL

MAJOR ATRIUM   SERVICE ELEVATOR   LOADING DOCK

5

PERSONNEL ELEVATORS   GRADE LEVEL ENTRANCE   LECTURE HALL   LARGER NMR SUITE

6

7

4   Typical lab space with visual connection to circulation spaces

5   Floor plan

6   Overview of the light-filled atrium

7   Meeting rooms and offices overlook social space

8   Interior atrium delivers natural light throughout lab facility

8

9

9 Welcoming staircase also contains areas where one can sit, rest and socialize

10 Festive tables with umbrellas invite staff and scientists to interact informally

11 Large skylights fill the atrium with natural illumination

12 Lab spaces are found directly off of circulation links, such as staircases

Photography: Steve Hall/Hedrich-Blessing

10

11

12

1

2

3

This project for the Portland, Oregon, Bureau of Environmental Services is situated along the Willamette River at the base of the St. John's Bridge. The facility returns a 7.6-acre industrial site that was once polluted to public access, and includes a state-of-the-art-testing laboratory, offices, community use meeting rooms, and an outdoor storm water demonstration garden. Water run-off from the St. John's neighborhood is treated on site in the water demonstration retention pond. A waterfront pathway connects the adjacent Cathedral Park and invites visitors to experience this unique facility.

One of the main priorities of the project was to maximize natural light and provide connections to the scenic surroundings of the park, river, and hillsides for employees. Ergonomically designed open office areas utilize system furniture with glazed panels. Glass-walled private offices and meeting rooms are placed along the core. The results are natural light filtering throughout the interior of the 37,626-square-foot building and river views for all. The building's form and the choice of materials and colors reflect the strong imagery of the St. John's Bridge and the organic nature of the client's mission. Deep overhangs, sunscreens, and shade trees reduce interior heat gain.

To enhance a healthy environment, the facility utilizes operable windows. Computerized interior window shades and an energy-efficient lighting system minimize internal heat load and help reduce overall energy use. The laboratory systems provide 100 percent outside air for ventilation, conditioned by a single two-stage, direct/indirect evaporative cooling system. Heat recovery is provided by a closed glycol/water loop between exhaust air systems and outside air.

1   Colorful entry to lab echoes architecture of bridge
2   Sunshades help mitigate solar heat gain and reduce glare
3   View of the lab building as it faces the water

WATER POLLUTION CONTROL LABORATORY

SERA ARCHITECTS AND
MILLER|HULL PARTNERSHIP

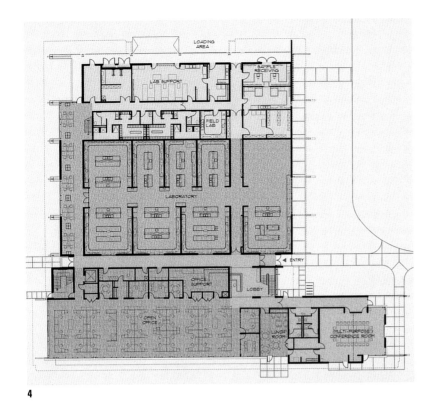

4

6

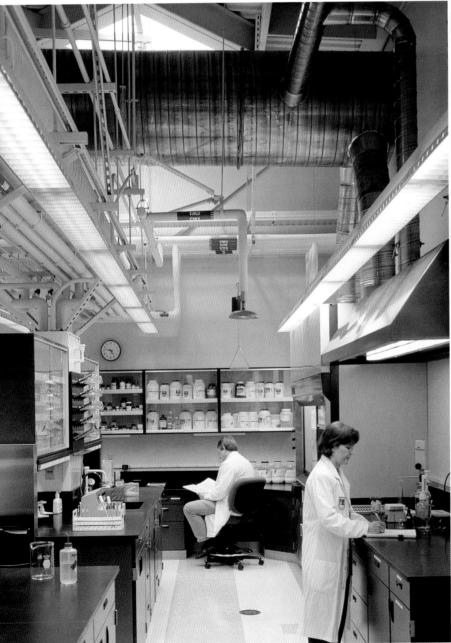

5

7

4   Floor plan

5   Lab areas have high ceilings to accommodate equipment

6   Work area offers sweeping views of the river

7   Landscaped areas offer places to relax for lab workers and staff

8   Lab as it sits in its natural setting, its architecture blending with landscape

Photography: Stode Eckert Photographic

8

1

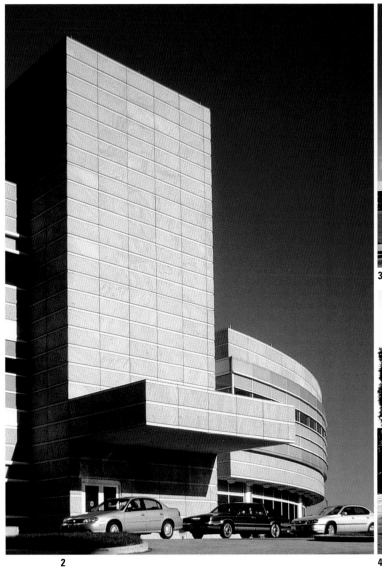

2

3

4

Part of the expanding Cleveland Clinic Foundation campus, the new Cole Eye Institute is sited adjacent to the Crile Clinic Building (designed by Cesar Pelli & Associates in 1984) and houses the Division of Ophthalmology. The new building provides state-of-the-art facilities with potential for future expansion, and encourages interaction and collaboration among physicians and scientists.

The four-story, 130,000-square-foot building includes ambulatory surgery, research laboratories, diagnostic services, continuing education, refractive surgery, pediatric treatment and a research library. For the first time, the Division of Ophthalmology connects clinical work with laboratory research in one building. These adjacencies are mutually beneficial, allowing for association of various disciplines. Conference rooms and a three-story skylit atrium with balconies not only foster the exchange of ideas but are welcoming environments for patients.

Following the objectives of the masterplan, the new building improves the public image of the Foundation on one of the city's major corridors, Euclid Avenue, by delineating a clear eastern border for the campus. It forms a new entrance to the campus and acts as a highly visible gateway for visitors approaching Cleveland from the east. At the same time, the Cole Eye Institute defines the edge of a future garden courtyard on the campus side, the East Campus Quadrangle. This public open space will be framed on the north side by the Institute, on the west by the Crile Clinic, and on the east by the future East 105th Street Parking Garage.

The Cole Eye Institute is integrated into the campus' architectural style yet has its own recognizable identity. This granite building, compatible with its neighbors, complements the character and style of other campus buildings of distinction. The massing of the building directly addresses the duality of the site, acknowledging its function as a gateway between the public and private realms.

1   Eye Institute in its Cleveland context
2   Drop-off area at the building's narrow end
3   Building's sweeping geometry makes it a landmark
4   Institute as it faces main thoroughfare

COLE EYE INSTITUTE

CESAR PELLI & ASSOCIATES

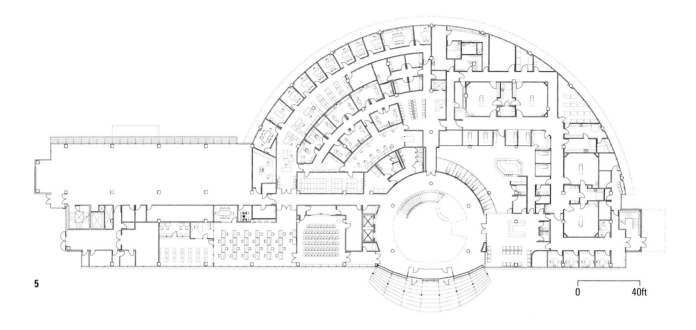

5

0   40ft

6

7

8

9

5　Floor plan
6　Sweeping lobby recalls geometry of building's exterior
7　Floor design extends the circular, spiral theme
8　Frit-coated glass helps to mitigate glare
9　Natural light is used throughout interior spaces
Photography: Jeff Goldberg/Esto

1

2

3

4

5

The Institute for Forestry and Nature Research (IBN) in Wageningen, The Netherlands, sought what it called a 'human and environmentally friendly building for the future' that used durable and sustainable building techniques and strategies, without incurring extra costs.

Natural woods and other materials were chosen for their environmental and cost benefits. High-performance insulation and glazing, ventilation and natural cooling were also used. Covered gardens serve alternately as energy-efficient, green working places and relaxation gardens. The 121,000-square-foot building's carefully cultivated, yet edgy, scrappiness rises above its functional, organic gardens.

IBN desired a building with a closed water cycle, so roofs and terraces were designed to collect rainwater in a retaining pond in the north, where plants (heliophites) naturally purify the runoff. State building department experts used new analytical and statistical calculations to compare the materials and systems used in the building to conventional alternatives, measuring the alternatives in terms of energy consumption of the building, embodied energy of materials and systems, and the environmental impact of demolishing and recycling the building.

The design conveys a sense of being sheltered in nature. Offices adjacent to covered gardens (on upper levels) have a gallery for secondary routing, allowing the office space to extend into the covered garden. A library, conference center, and cafeteria are located at the south end of the office wings for easy access from anywhere in the complex.

The landscape design allows plants and trees to naturally occur and animals to populate over time. Elements such as stone walls, trees, hedges, berms, ponds, swamps, tree lanes, and water channels create a green belt linking a nearby nature reserve park in the east to the Rhine valleys in the west.

1 Building incorporates colors found in natural landscape
2 Façade of building as it faces the water
3 Lush greenery is found throughout interior atrium
4 Lab complex is a visually permeable building
5 Interior offers a multitude of opportunities for respite from work

INSTITUTE FOR FORESTRY AND NATURE RESEARCH

BEHNISCH, BEHNISCH & PARTNER

6

7

8

9

6   Circulation is via open balconies that line the interior

7   Lounges and terraces overlook sun-filled, green spaces

8   View from garden toward labs and offices

9   Bold colors are found inside to enliven environment

10   Overview of interior atrium with adjustable glazing system

Photography: Martin Schodder/Christian Kandzia

10

The Harvey W. Wiley Federal Building forms part of the consolidation and renewal of the U.S. Food and Drug Administration facilities in the Washington D.C. region. Located in College Park, Maryland, the new home for the Center for Food Safety and Applied Nutrition brings together previously disparate offices, providing state-of-the-art facilities for integrated laboratory and office work, and creates space for joint efforts between the FDA and the University of Maryland at College Park.

Primary goals were to provide facilities suitable for a first-rate, scientific organization to inspire research and review work and to support recruitment and interaction with international agencies such as the World Health Organization. The mandate for the design was to bring together lab research and office review procedures and thus integrate the entire facility and its working population.

The 410,000-square-foot program called for labs, offices, and support facilities. Additional program elements included food service, a library, a fitness center, training rooms, and an auditorium. In anticipation of further consolidation, expansion of laboratories equal to the initial lab component was developed on the site.

Integration of the different spaces is achieved by creating a common sky-lit atrium with laboratories and offices on facing sides and an open library on its ground floor level. Laboratories link to the surrounding office wings on each end. Glazed openings provide visual connections, while common shared 'task force' rooms are located at the points of connection of labs and offices.

Public elevators and stairs lead to balconies within the common atrium space, providing visibility between labs and offices, and of people moving through the building. The open atrium library, with a large component of current periodicals, acts as a meeting space, visible to adjacent occupants, but separated at ground level by shoulder-height bookcases.

Opposite:
North façade, which contains offices, bends slightly

HARVEY W. WILEY FEDERAL BUILDING

CENTER FOR FOOD SAFETY & NUTRITION

KALLMANN MCKINNELL & WOOD

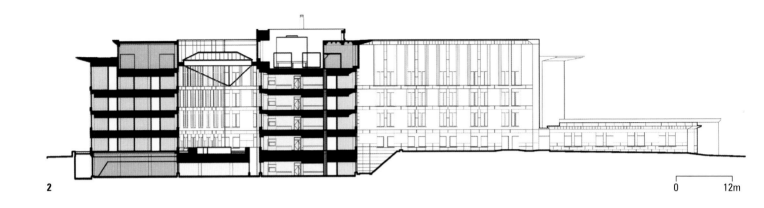

2

0   12m

3

2   Section through atrium

3   Building's north elevation is lifted by its aerodynamic roof

4   Detail of the building's sleek, elegantly detailed corner

5   Light-colored building sits atop a base of dark stone

4

5

7

Opposite:
    Atrium is the physical and social heart of the building

7 Typical lab spaces are simple and straightforward

8 Ground floor of atrium houses the facility's library

Photography: Robert Benson Photography

8

1

2

The renovation of the Searles Science Building on Bowdoin's Brunswick, Maine, campus demonstrates how significant, older buildings can be successfully revitalized to accommodate technology, accessibility, and modern function, while preserving their historic qualities.

Searles had housed Chemistry, Biology, and Physics since its completion in 1894. As the new center for Physics, Mathematics, and Computer Science, Searles brings together the college's most intensive users of digital information. Renovation work focused on reallocating functions to better utilize the existing spaces and increase classroom space, simplify and clarify circulation, and integrate flexibility and new technology.

A light-filled, 2,000-square-foot, three-story infill addition connects two wings on the street-side of the building. This promotes communication between floors and departments, and provides a new common space and circulation spine, accessibility throughout, and a new front entrance on the street. Clad in lead-coated copper and punctuated with large glass windows to create a reserved, modern statement, the addition also allows the historic building to dominate and retain its historic character on the quadrangle.

Structural steel supports for the stairway and stainless steel brackets for glass panel railings are modern in spirit. Renovation work visually emphasizes flexibility and audiovisual communications, computer systems, and wiring. Cable trays above the ceilings in the corridors provide connections to each room, while a brushed aluminum conduit box runs along the perimeter of the rooms at chair-rail height.

Based on work sessions with faculty and users, computer labs and classrooms are paired at each end of the bridge to increase efficiency, allowing one class to use both rooms. The large, second floor lecture hall was divided into a classroom/seminar room, taking advantage of a central high window and internal space dedicated as a computer lab. The infusion of abundant light into the building enhances the sense of community nurtured by the integration of program, department, and student space.

1   View from Maine Street to restored building with new infill addition
2   Street elevation

SEARLES SCIENCE BUILDING

BOWDOIN COLLEGE

CAMBRIDGE SEVEN ASSOCIATES, INC.

Opposite:
Detail of new metal-clad addition to older brick structure

4   First floor plan

5   Infill creates new connections and spaces for informal interaction

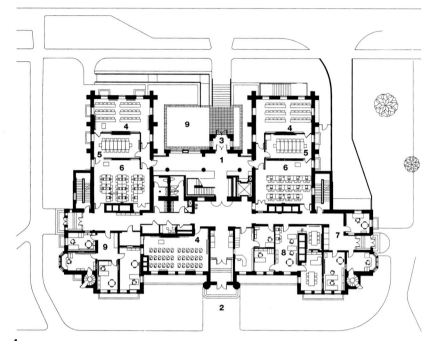

1   New central atrium
2   Existing entry
3   New entry
4   Classroom
5   Seminar
6   Lab
7   Offices
8   Skills center
9   Outdoor class space

4

5

6

7

8

6   Light is used in hallways to expand the sense of space

7   Physics laboratory was relocated to upper floor under vintage wood structure

8   New lecture hall brings students through building to upper floors

Photography: Steve Rosenthal

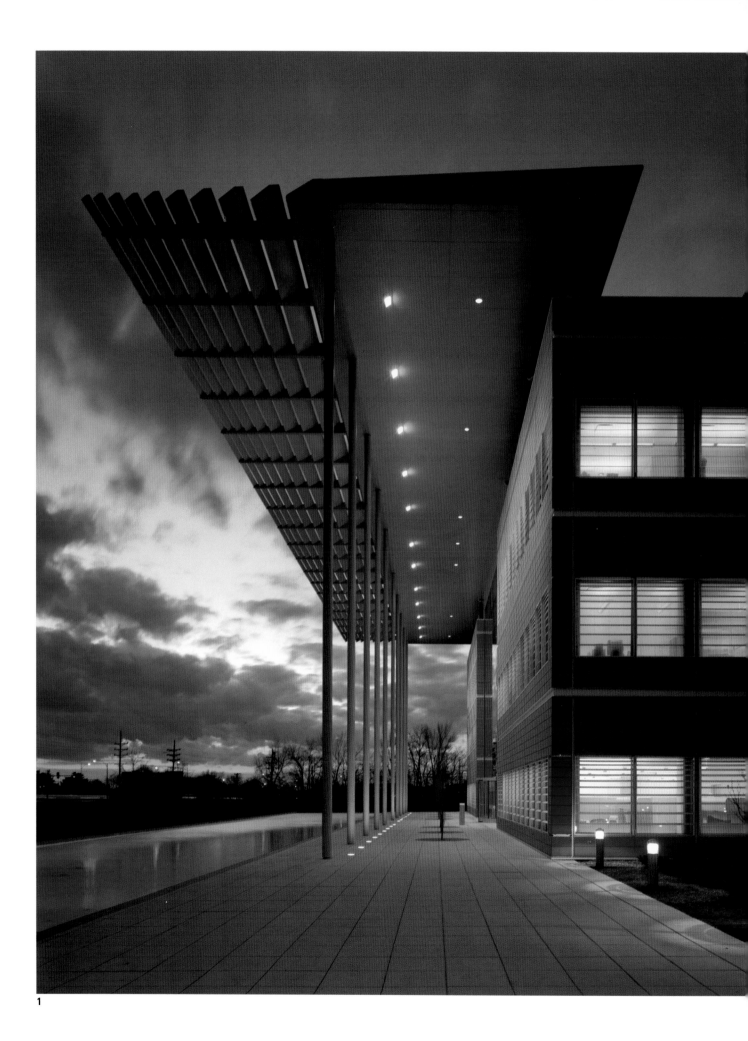

The Donald Danforth Plant Science Center is an independent, not-for-profit research facility for the use of both scientists and laypeople dedicated to advancing the understanding of the world's reliance on plants. The center is located on a 40-acre site in suburban Creve Coeur, Missouri, about 10 miles from St. Louis.

The varied operations of the building are arranged into layers to create a passive separation between the public and private functions, thus providing an open working environment with a community atmosphere. Laboratories and offices are arranged into two main wings, each comprising 11,000 square feet of useable space. The wings are separated by a central 9500-square-foot atrium, and linked by a series of walkways, bridges, and meeting platforms providing a semi-private space for informal meetings. Both have access to the freestanding 'pod' at the southern end of the building footprint, containing the semi-public areas of the library, meeting rooms, and faculty lounge. A 300-seat auditorium and a café are in the basement.

The atrium, with its ridged north-light roof and two structural glass curtain wall end elevations, is a light and airy internal garden. It provides a balance between the fully air-conditioned lab areas and the outside environment, helping to reduce operating costs. The building layers are further extended out into the environment along its south elevation by an external public space or 'front street.' This street is flanked on one side by the south face of the building and on the other by a narrow reflecting pond. Care has been taken to use low-embodied energy materials in the building. A terra cotta rain screen curtain wall with integral aluminum sun-shading louvers tempers the effects of the environment on the east and west faces of the building envelope.

DONALD DANFORTH PLANT SCIENCE CENTER

GRIMSHAW

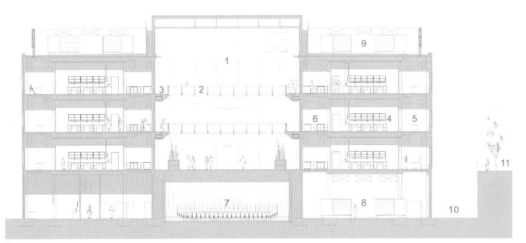

2

3

1 Atrium	**7 Auditorium**
2 Bridge	**8 Plant room**
3 Walkway	**9 Plant**
4 Laboratories	**10 Service area**
5 Scientists' lab offices	**11 Parking**
6 Lab support	

2 Cross section looking north

3 South elevation is distinguished by a canopy, overlooking the reflecting pool

4 Atrium space near the north entry, with connecting bridge at right

5 View of atrium looking south, with saw-tooth roof above

6 Levels two and three

7 Lab spaces receive borrowed light from offices at periphery

Photography: Timothy Hursley

4

5

1 Laboratories
2 Scientists' lab offices
3 Lab support
4 Administration suite
5 Library
6 Elevator
7 Service elevator
8 Media kitchen
9 Atrium void
10 Bridge
11 Meeting area

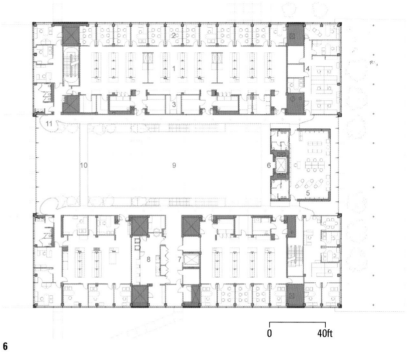

0   40ft

6

7

67

1

2

The renovation of the Dorrance and Whitaker Buildings on the MIT campus in Cambridge, Massachusetts, creates a major new laboratory facility that celebrates the integration of art, architecture, and technology. Constructed in 1953 and 1964, respectively, as connected research laboratories, the two buildings now house the offices, classrooms, and laboratories of more than two dozen departments, including chemistry, chemical engineering, toxicology, and biotechnology. The many classrooms and seminar rooms have been designed to integrate information and presentation technologies. Students' and instructors' desks are fully networked and integrated with the extensive information network facilities of the Institute. Laboratories, with custom-designed modular bench systems, are adapted to the specific needs of diverse users and provide flexibility for a broad range of current and future uses. Benches have also been oriented to maximize the light and view provided by the extensive curtain wall.

The Dorrance and Whitaker Buildings are an important link along MIT's 'infinite corridor' of interconnected buildings. The challenge was to transform a particularly dreary stretch of this corridor into a lively high-tech street. Fiber-optic, edge-lit glass sculpture, a light-emitting diode information board, and a video projection wall with interactive media art displays animate the ground floor. Patterned terrazzo floors, inspired by fractal geometry, reflect patterns of movement through the space, adding visual excitement to the lobbies. The fiber-optic, edge-lit glass display distinguishes the threshold between the buildings.

While the interior renovation made the Dorrance and Whitaker Buildings more visually and socially appealing, the exterior renovation reorganized and updated the buildings' drab façade. Renovations to the metal and glass curtain wall increased the buildings' transparency without upstaging their neighbors. The architects applied waterproofing treatments and added custom mullion caps to make the façade more graphically distinctive while skillfully concealing the waterproofing system.

1 New entry vestibule, receiving/waste facility, and elevator tower are expressed as delicate, contemporary elements

2 Custom-designed mullion caps and new metal infill panels in the original curtain wall were painted to blend this façade with the surrounding limestone and concrete buildings

DORRANCE AND WHITAKER BUILDINGS

MASSACHUSETTS INSTITUTE OF TECHNOLOGY

ELLENZWEIG ASSOCIATES

4

5

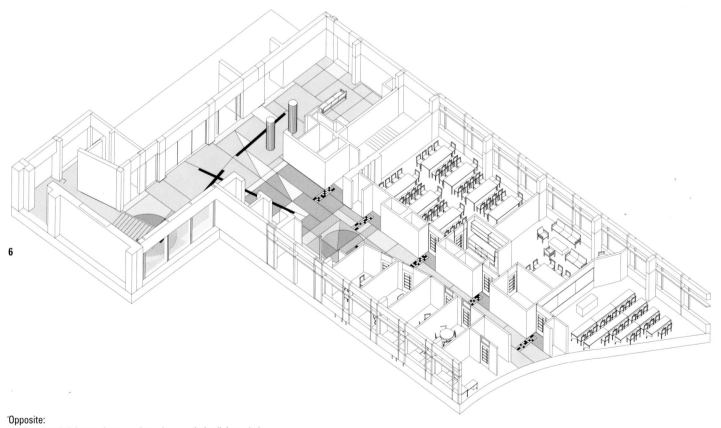

6

'Opposite:
Benches in laboratories are oriented to maximize light and views

4 Institute's state-of-the-art computer network is exposed to the corridor through a custom-design steel frame window system

5 Classroom entry features a natural ash door and blue opaque glass in custom-designed steel frames

6 Axonometric

7

8

7 Terrazzo floor in main lobby reflects the patterns of movement through the space while the media wall presents a dynamic visual display of light and graphics

8 Classrooms have been designed with students' and instructors' desks fully networked and integrated with the extensive audio-visual facilities of the institute

9 Although designed around a standard modular system, the laboratories are flexible enough to accommodate changes in future use

10 Stainless steel column enclosures conceal existing concrete structure while the fiber-optic edge-lit glass walls announce the transition into the adjoining building

Photography: Steve Rosenthal

9

This new science center is designed to encourage interaction among scientists from across the university. Duke's renowned Collegiate Gothic campus in Durham, North Carolina, with its courtyards and gray stone cladding, inspired the architecture of the new building.

The science center defines two new campus spaces: the school for the environment courtyard and the main quad. An 800-foot-long arcade connects the two spaces with a ground level café acting as a filter between the two courtyards. Service access is shielded from the campus along the north face of the building.

The science center includes a 300-seat auditorium and conference rooms. Facilities are designed to promote the exchange of ideas through university-wide, national, and international seminars and conferences. All of Duke's science departments meet and merge at the main entrance lobby, a grand space known as the 'Hall of Science.' Here are found the shared amenities of a café, conference rooms, informal lounges, and a central stair. Each department and the auditorium has an entry off this central space. The auditorium entry, located off the main staircase mid-landing, is the most prominent threshold in the Hall of Science. The central café serves as a daily meeting place for faculty, students, and visiting scholars from both the center and the science and engineering buildings surrounding it.

The exterior's beige and gray precast concrete accented by blue-painted steel evokes the flavor of Duke's main campus. Additionally, the use of clear glass windows, entrance towers, grouped chimneys, and other Gothic-inspired elements reinforce this connection. Landscape elements such as low stone walls and plantings help meld the new building with the existing science buildings. The new center's configuration on the site creates private pockets of outdoor space, some of which can be used as outdoor classrooms.

LEVINE SCIENCE RESEARCH CENTER

DUKE UNIVERSITY

PAYETTE ASSOCIATES

2 Exterior design was inspired by Gothic style of the Duke campus

3 Storage and shelving is incorporated into bench design

4 Large auditorium is at the heart of the building, where it is easily accessed

5 Floor plan

2

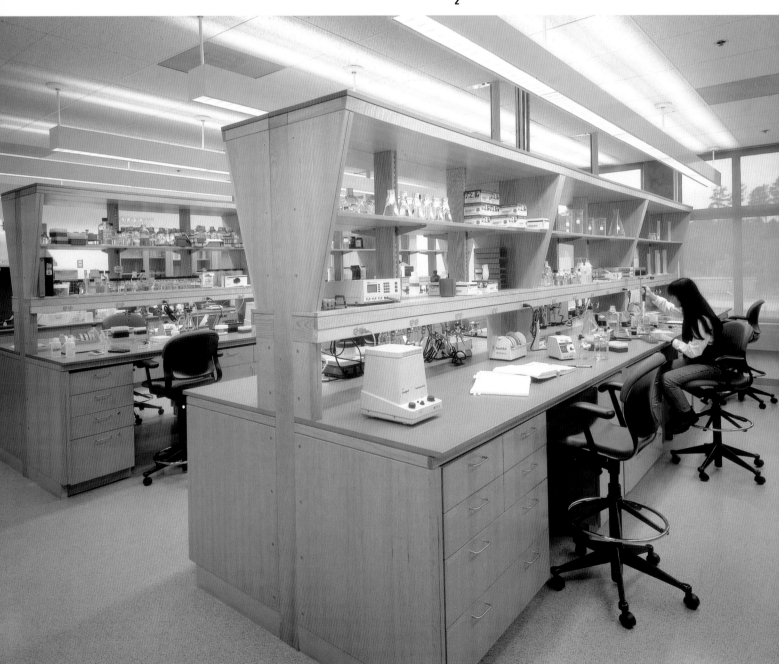

3

4

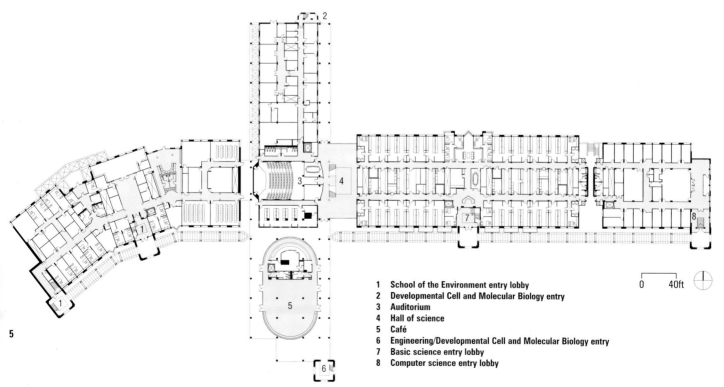

1   School of the Environment entry lobby
2   Developmental Cell and Molecular Biology entry
3   Auditorium
4   Hall of science
5   Café
6   Engineering/Developmental Cell and Molecular Biology entry
7   Basic science entry lobby
8   Computer science entry lobby

0   40ft

5

6   Lab work areas are flooded with natural light

7   Library space has glazed walls for visual connections

8   Central stair is part of building's 'Hall of Science'

9   View down the long arcade that stretches along building's south façade

Photography: Brian Vanden Brink

6

8

9

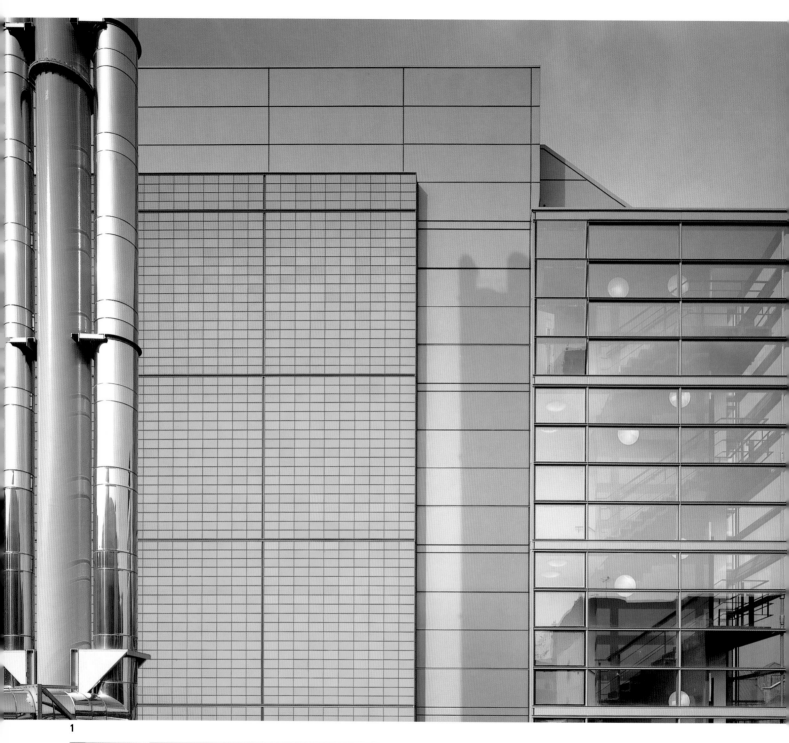

1

2

1 Cladding is a combination of complementary materials

2 Interior woodwork and furnishings complement exterior materials

The Institute of Reproductive & Developmental Biology research lab is located on a tight site on the Hammersmith Hospital Campus in West London. This 36,000-square-foot, six-story facility is for the Obstetrics & Gynecology Department at the Imperial College of Science, Technology, and Medicine. Working with Professor Lord Winston, the designers provided a flexible modular laboratory environment with attractive office and social spaces. The design is integrated both internally and externally, with the organization of spaces reflected in the architecture of the façade. The laboratory and support zones are articulated in the terra cotta cladding, while the offices and write-up areas are expressed more lightly with the north-facing glazed, transparent façades overlooking a landscaped courtyard and open areas beyond.

The layouts are clearly zoned, distinguishing the open laboratories and support space from the write-up and office space, and providing a variety of spatial areas within the working environment. The main circulation spine on each typical laboratory floor separates the lab zone from the office and write-up zone. The vertical circulation and mechanical cores are arranged on the east and west flanks of the building. These cores are connected to the mechanical plant located in a penthouse at roof level.

The ground floor incorporates the social, meeting, and administrative areas. The main entrance is combined with a social space and addresses a landscaped courtyard providing an internal forum where the research scientists can meet and an arrival point for visitors to the facility. A lecture space for 40 to 50 people is adjacent to this space.

INSTITUTE OF REPRODUCTIVE & DEVELOPMENTAL BIOLOGY

IMPERIAL COLLEGE OF SCIENCE, TECHNOLOGY, AND MEDICINE

ANSHEN+ALLEN

Opposite:
 Ample, sunlit staircases attract staff use, encouraging collaboration

4 Lounge area is rendered in warm wood for welcoming atmosphere

5 Section

Photography: John Edward Linden Photography

4

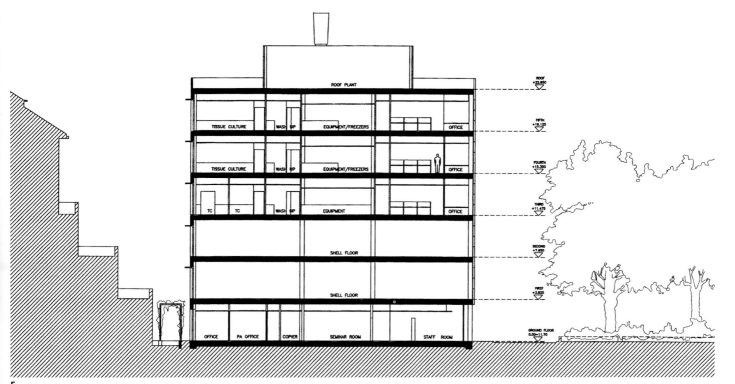

5

This second building of the Becton Dickinson campus in Franklin Lakes, New Jersey, houses in its 450,000 square feet the Divisional Headquarters' offices and research laboratories that complement the Corporate Headquarters built five years earlier, and further develops the architectural theme of a workplace in a country setting.

Like its predecessor, the new building is laid out as a low, extended structure with its wings stretching out in a finger-like arrangement northwards into the site, allowing for a majority of offices to be placed along its exterior walls. Since these offices do not have doors, the adjacent interior workspaces can also enjoy views of the landscape. A transverse concourse provides access to all the fingers of the plan. It joins the three atria, each designed with different materials and a different ambience, and connects the three major staircases for vertical interaction. The two longer fingers of the plan enclose a block of vertically stacked laboratories, while two of the shorter fingers contain a cafeteria, private dining, and classrooms. A knuckle placed slightly off-center houses the entry, lobby, grand staircase and loggia, and a lecture hall amphitheatre below. Garden terraces are laid out as bas-relief in collaboration with the sculptor Michael Singer.

The architectural language and materials of the building follow the precedent of the earlier building's planar form and the tectonic elements of walls, columns, window assemblies, and roof overhangs. The honey-colored brick and granite base, the limestone-framed windows, copper roof, and bracket supports are common to both buildings. The continuity between the two buildings on either side of the central lawn remains clearly established.

Opposite:
Vertical circulation is found near interior atrium spaces

DIVISIONAL HEADQUARTERS AND LABORATORIES

BECTON DICKINSON AND COMPANY

KALLMANN MCKINNELL & WOOD

2

3

2   Glass doors of private offices on periphery allow natural light to penetrate interior

3   Large windows are used in private offices to maximize light

4   Lab hallways contain open conduit and trays for plumbing, electrical, and computer cabling

5   Floor plan

4

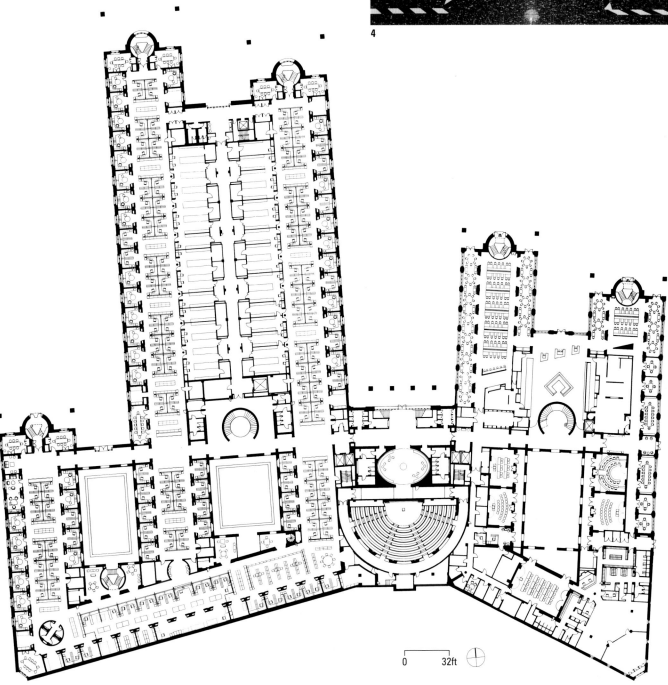

0   32ft

5

7

Opposite:
Typical laboratory interior, with exposed mechanical equipment

7   Lecture hall is simple in detail and materials

8   Glass doors permit lab observation from office areas

Photography: Robert Benson (2,3), Steve Rosenthal (p.84,7,8)
Peter Vanderwarker (4,opposite)

8

1

2

The Estuarine Habitats & Coastal Fisheries Center (EH&CFC) creates, in conjunction with the National Wetlands Research Center (NWRC), the beginnings of a university research campus in Lafayette, Louisiana dedicated to the study of coastal marine life and their habitats.

The program for this 67,000-square-foot facility includes a conference center, wet and dry laboratories, and administrative and research offices for the National Marine Fisheries Service, the U.S. Fish & Wildlife Service, the Corps of Engineers, and the Smithsonian Institution.

Two critical spaces were added during the design phase: an interpretive gallery, which serves to present the mission of the center to the visiting public, and a two-story 'commons,' which promotes interaction among the center's various users, becoming the social heart of the facility. Arranging the program into two distinct wings resulted from a careful analysis of user needs and cost/energy efficiencies related to the mix of office and laboratory system requirements.

The building's organization is visually expressed in the architectural treatment of the various spaces on the exterior. Offices are clad in metal panels, a lighter material indicating their dynamic and changeable nature while the more fixed public and laboratory spaces are solidly clad in brick masonry. The southwest elevation overlooks a man-made wetlands habitat. Here the metal face of the office wing is designed as a *brise-soleil* to protect windows from the harsh afternoon sun while also reflecting daylight deep into the offices for energy efficiency. The interpretive gallery is the most expressive element of the design, announcing itself as the primary public space of the facility. A metal shingle clad 'light box' extends outward to capture a small reflecting pool, which projects the play of light on water into the room and connects the space to the larger habitat just outside.

1   View looking north across wetlands habitat
2   Entry court with pool

ESTUARINE HABITATS & COASTAL FISHERIES CENTER

E S K E W   +   D U M E Z   +   R I P P L E

4

5

Opposite:
Interior detailing is crisp and elegant

4   Entry court features shaded promenade to main doors

5   View from the interpretive gallery

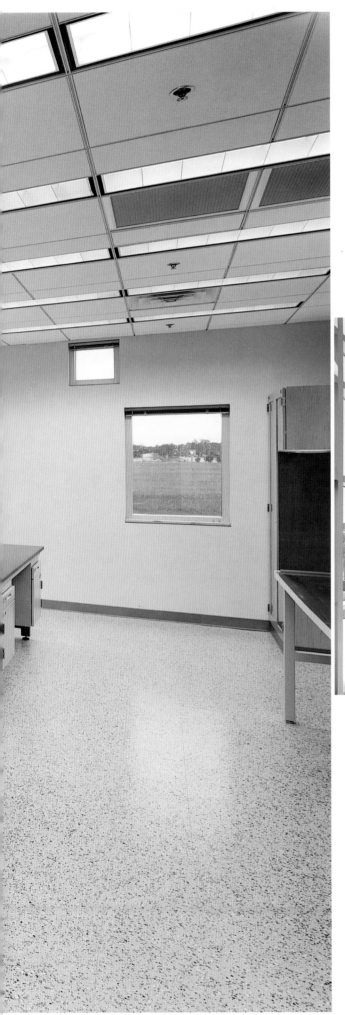

6   Typical laboratory layout

7   View from lobby toward interpretive center

8   Entry lobby is a glassy corridor linking wings

Photography: Timothy Hursley

7

8

95

1

2

This new teaching and research building for the Departments of Physics/Astronomy and Mathematics/Computer Science encourages interdisciplinary studies in a state-of-the-art facility that provides for advanced instructional technology and interactive pedagogy. The building houses teaching and research laboratories, classrooms and lecture halls, conference and seminar rooms, faculty offices, and a reading room/library, as well as a planetarium and observatory. The L-shaped building plan reflects the programmatic allocation of Physics/Astronomy in one wing, and Math/Computer Science in another, and provides shared spaces at the intersection of the two, where the wings embrace a garden space on Dickinson's Carlisle, Pennsylvania, campus.

On the exterior, the building utilizes the predominant campus material—a local limestone—on the campus or 'public' façades, celebrating the building's mission by expressing important program elements such as the planetarium, observatory, lecture hall, and library. The lecture hall and library are contained in an angled stone-clad form at one end, and the planetarium and observatory are located at the other in a dramatic metal-clad conical form, contrasting with the rough-hewn stone. The observatory sits atop the planetarium, and both components are isolated from the main building structure by a delicate glass lobby; this placement serves to eliminate vibrations. The separate entrance lobby to the planetarium allows access for off-campus groups without necessitating entry into the main building. Stucco is used on the 'private' garden façades. This side of the building faces away from the campus, defining an enclosed exterior space featuring an outdoor classroom. A balcony provides a welcoming outdoor space accessible from the second floor and accommodates substantial outdoor seating, while an overhead trellis provides a sense of enclosure.

Inside, the main stairway, with a wood paneling backdrop, provides a focal point for internal building circulation, while the library has a soaring ceiling and large windows for abundant natural light. Specialized physics laboratories support Dickinson's nationally acclaimed 'Workshop Physics' collaborative model—emphasizing hands-on, interactive learning—with central demonstration areas surrounded by T-shaped benches functioning alternately for experiments and shared computer operations. Similar interactive classrooms are provided for mathematics and computer science.

1   Glass lobby provides an independent, after-hours entry point to the planetarium, and forms a bridge to the observatory at roof level

2   Two wings of the L-shaped building are connected at the library (center); planetarium/observatory is at left

TOME MULTIDISCIPLINARY SCIENCE BUILDING

DICKINSON COLLEGE

ELLENZWEIG ASSOCIATES

3

3   Separate planetarium lobby is at center, communicating stair at left

4   Elevation

5   Outdoor space at second floor provides a pleasant area for meeting and informal dining, accessible from second floor lounge

6   Access to observatory is via the open bridge over planetarium lobby

7   Communicating stair is at left, the outdoor teaching area at right foreground; the metal-clad surface at lower right provides a slate writing surface on the opposite side for use in the outdoor classroom

8   Floor plan

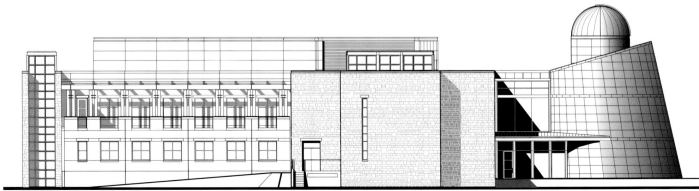

4

5

6

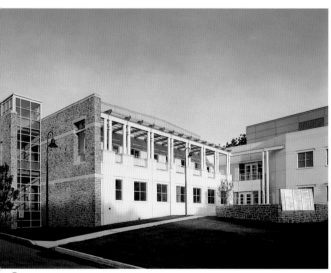

7

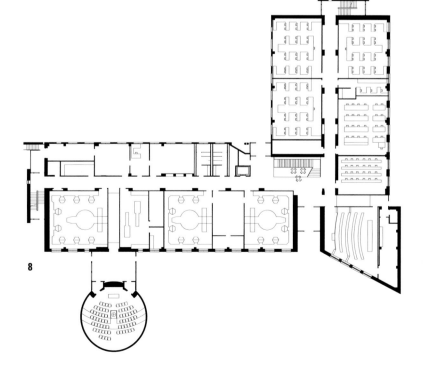

8

99

10

Opposite:
  Angled ceiling of library rises toward large windows on one side, providing an abundance of natural light for reading areas

10 Math lab's flexible teaching spaces allow for traditional lectures, shared computer use, and group activities

11 Each workshop physics lab has an open area for demonstrations and flexible tables on the perimeter; hexagonal tables can be re-configured for a variety of class functions

12 Lecture hall has continuous table seating with data and power connections at each seat; a multifunctional demonstration bench provides access to all room controls

Photography: Tom Crane (1), Anton Grassl (2,3,5–11)

11

12

1   Entry to the building is found on its narrow end—common to many lab facilities

The directive from Bayer for this project in West Haven, Connecticut, was to 'design a building for chemistry research that is ultimately flexible and provides an image statement for chemistry research unmatched in the world.' The architects worked closely with users and facilities staff to create spaces that allow the integration of analytical groups and combinatorial techniques common in the research. The hope is to encourage interdisciplinary collaboration at the discovery level and to accelerate the product-to-market cycle.

Another motive behind the design was to compete more effectively for top research talent. A recent national trend in new chemistry space and a subsequent increase in hiring meant Bayer needed its new facility to be even more competitive in retaining existing staff and attracting new hires. The new facility has increased retention rates for chemists by 50 percent in a highly competitive market.

Building B27 consists of three floors of labs, basement support, and a penthouse. The 125,000-square-foot building is organized around the typical laboratory module. The entire lab can be configured to just about any type of workspace. Lab offices are located along the perimeter wall. The design promotes cross-communication among staff, while related disciplines are grouped together to encourage interaction and communication.

Exterior elements such as brick and pre-cast concrete allow Building B27 to fit contextually into the Bayer campus.

In addition to helping Bayer retain the chemists it already employs, Bayer reports that the building has helped to recruit new researchers. Before it opened, one researcher accepted a job at Bayer for every four offers made. Since its completion, the ratio has increased to one in three.

BAYER BUILDING B27

FLAD ASSOCIATES

2

3

2   Light materials and soft forms complement glass façade

3   Darker woods are used to distinguish conference room

4   Site plan

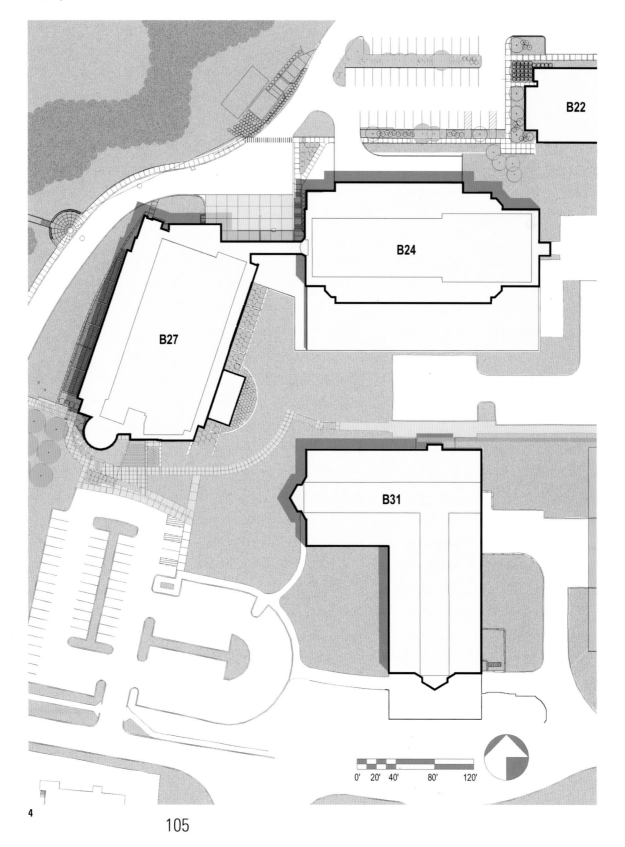

4

5

5   Moveable equipment allows the lab to be reconfigured as research needs change

6   Typical interior corridor of lab space

7   Typical lab layout with built-in fume hoods

Photography: Steve Hall/Hedrich-Blessing

7

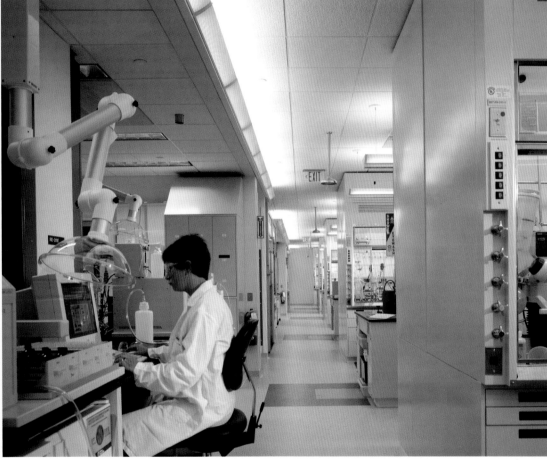

6

107

The renovation of Doherty Hall on Carnegie Mellon's Pittsburgh, Pennsylvania, campus into interdisciplinary undergraduate science laboratories involved upgrading an historic 1908 building and a thorough evaluation of emerging pedagogical methods on the design of laboratories, classrooms, and public areas.

The process-based teaching and student research conducted in the laboratories suggested that well equipped, fixed student work stations would be preferable to moveable student stations. Instrumentation was then placed on moveable carts that could be docked at any of the stations during lab hours. Central instrumentation rooms with overhead utility wings support the equipment when it is not in use in the labs.

Fume hoods and casework were configured to allow pairs of students to work together during any given lab period without having to compete for resources. Each team area contains a fume hood, local water source, multiple groups of utility connections, and seating areas for documentation or instrumentation docking. Student lockers housing individual equipment and experiments are located in each team designated space.

Lab casework is designed to maintain clear lines of sight around the labs for the professors and staff. Additionally, chemical transport is limited to a dedicated service elevator that can deliver chemicals and supplies from the main storeroom directly to the satellite storerooms on each lab floor.

Windows surrounding the labs on three sides provide abundant views and natural light. Adjustable, built-in stools are provided at seating areas at the end of each teaming location. Small, comfortable reference rooms are located off of each lab, and music is played over an individual system in each lab.

The façade of the addition takes its cues from the original building while striving to celebrate the functions it houses. The dominant element on the façade is a glazed area containing exhaust ductwork, which allows open floor areas within the chemistry laboratories (which was important to the chemistry department).

Opposite:
View of new wing as it connects to older building

INTERDISCIPLINARY UNDERGRADUATE SCIENCE LABORATORIES

CARNEGIE MELLON UNIVERSITY

BURT HILL KOSAR RITTELMANN ASSOCIATES

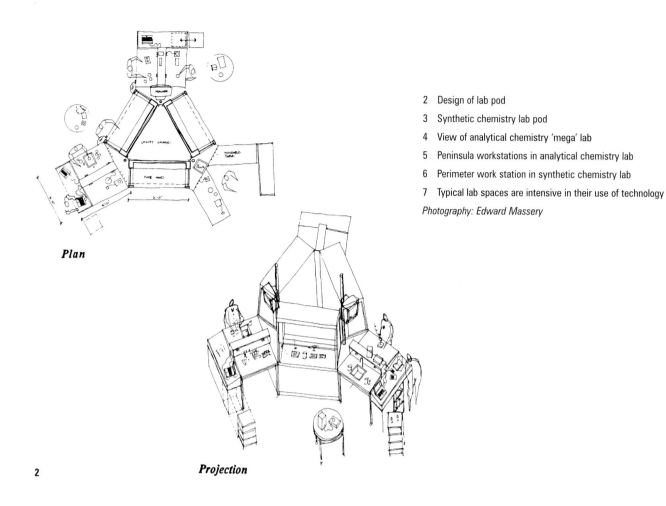

Plan

Projection

2

2　Design of lab pod
3　Synthetic chemistry lab pod
4　View of analytical chemistry 'mega' lab
5　Peninsula workstations in analytical chemistry lab
6　Perimeter work station in synthetic chemistry lab
7　Typical lab spaces are intensive in their use of technology

Photography: Edward Massery

3　　　　　　　　　　　　　　　　　　　　　　　4

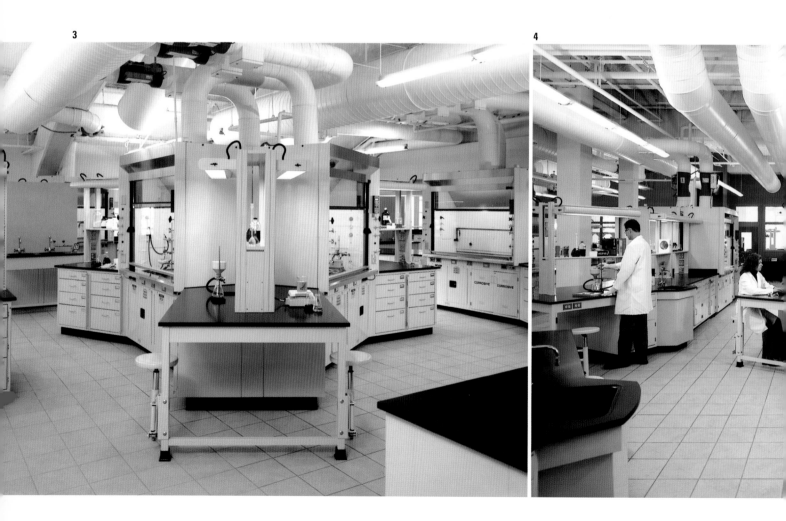

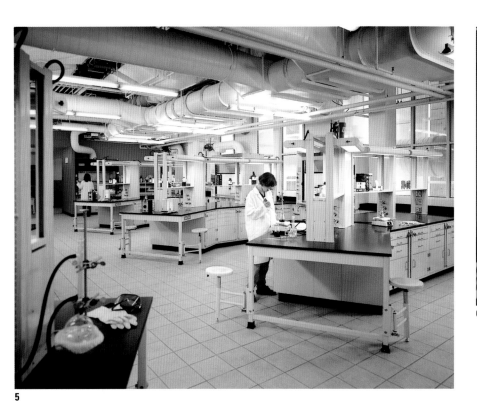

5

6

7

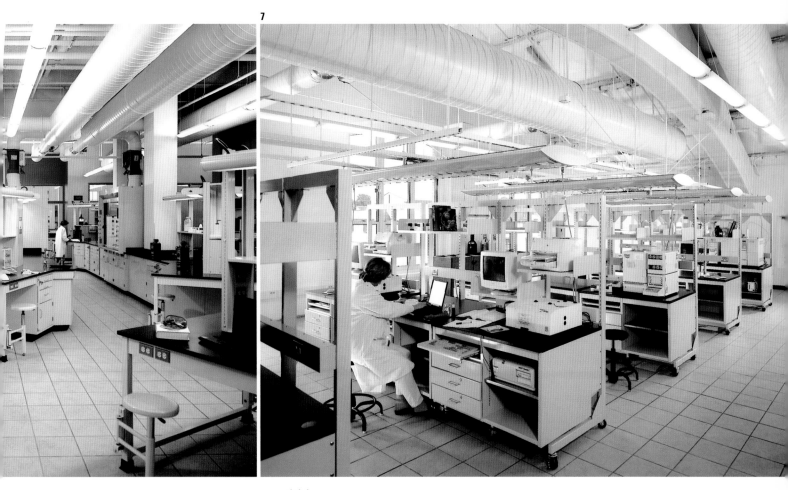

1 Building's curved forms provide a memorable image

2 Building has a strong presence along main thoroughfare

3 Night view of institute building in its Cleveland context

The new Lerner Research Institute in Cleveland, Ohio, is the Cleveland Clinic Foundation's center for biomedical research. Lerner is adjacent to the Crile Building, which is the focus of outpatient services at the Cleveland Clinic and was designed by Cesar Pelli & Associates in 1984.

Housing over 150,000 square feet of laboratory, support, and administrative space, the complex also includes 80,000 square feet of laboratories and research facilities for the Department of Biomedical Engineering, where the Clinic explores implant technologies and biomaterial science. The project features an enclosed public space, the Commons, facing a central courtyard where members of the Clinic community can meet informally.

The Education Institute, the primary teaching arm of the Foundation, is part of the same group of buildings and it comprises a 50,000-square-foot medical library, 40,000 square feet of teaching and conference facilities, and 40,000 square feet of administration and operations areas. The new library replaces an existing facility and includes a state-of-the-art medical research branch to serve the Foundation's research and clinical staff. Configured on two levels within the new Education Division headquarters, the library accommodates more than 44,000 active medical journals, on-line medical research data, and 12,000 additional medical titles. Approximately 1000 current medical journals, the heart of the materials provided by a medical library, are displayed for easy access to the users. Casual seating, carrels, and individual study rooms are provided with access to the campus data network from each study position. A computer demonstration classroom and an extensive audio-visual materials collection are also accommodated. Advanced video conferencing and telemedicine capabilities are incorporated throughout the teaching and conference facilities.

LERNER RESEARCH INSTITUTE

CESAR PELLI & ASSOCIATES

113

4

5

6

7

8

9

4 Welcoming staircase facilitates informal meetings of colleagues

5 Curved ceiling in informal gathering space

6 Façade elements help to break down this large building's scale

7 Curved element signals the building's entry

8 Shaded outdoor areas are welcoming gathering places

9 Double-height lounge spaces are filled with natural light

10 Fourth floor plan

Photography: Jeff Goldberg/Esto

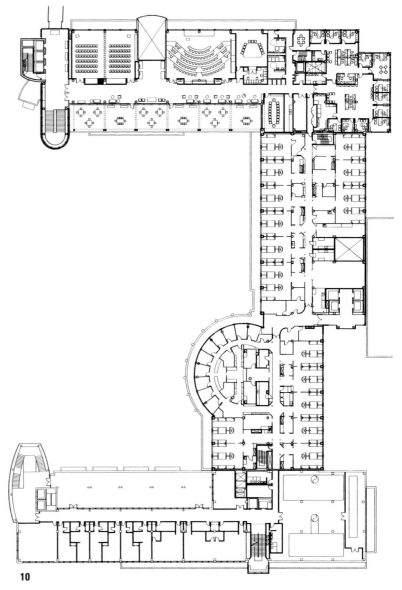

10

The new Hunts House responds to the complex constraints and opportunities provided by several urban design conditions. Sited in an historic London setting with a hospital on one side and the King's College medical campus on the other, its long narrow footprint re-establishes the historic presence of Old Hunts House (a facility it replaces) and the Memorial Quad as the heart of the medical school. Its massing and fenestration are designed to mediate between the larger urban scale of the hospital and the smaller pedestrian scale of the medical school, reinforcing existing campus edges, open spaces, and paths.

In a clear articulation of the building's most public functions, the lecture halls and information resources center are located to one end of the lower two floors of the five-story, 250,000-square-foot building. The primary entry is articulated as a more transparent, glass curtain wall opening to the campus quad along its most heavily trafficked pedestrian routes, essentially extending these spaces to the outdoors. A second more private entrance for the scientists and researchers is found in the middle of the building along with its core functions to separate the research and academic circulation paths. The core vertically leads to the more restricted research laboratories, offices, and smaller classrooms on the upper three floors and southern half of the building.

The top story of the façade overlooking the quad is set back and expressed in lighter materials than the brick face below, maintaining the height of the neighboring brick buildings. Rooftop services are placed up against the edge of the street façade where its larger mass is more appropriate to the scale of its urban surrounds and away from the intimate medical school.

Tower elements recall the varied roofscape of Old Hunts House, the new facility's predecessor, while punctuating the long linear façades. In addition to housing service and support functions, they provide highly visible, vertical, orienting elements that terminate visual axes extending beyond the site and demark principal entries.

HUNTS HOUSE

KING'S COLLEGE

ANSHEN+ALLEN

2

3

4

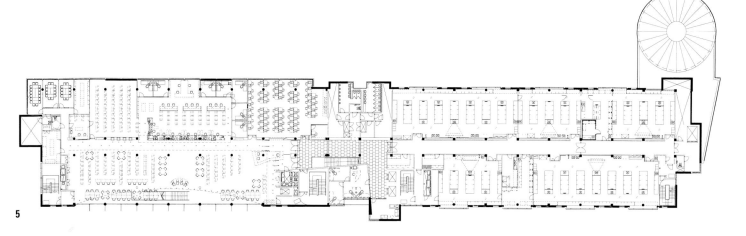

5

6

7

8

2   New building as it faces landscaped quad

3   Detail of façade, with its colorful glass fins

4   Detail of celebratory roof, with its crowning sunshades

5   Floor plan

6   View down lab corridor, with support spaces and offices to right

7   Light brick contrasts with darker curtainwall elements

8   Work areas in library arc gracefully along the window, exposing lower level

10

11

Opposite:
    Gracious stair in library, connecting levels

10   Light colors are used to enliven the building's public areas

11   Auditorium space offers natural materials accented with primary color

Photography: John Edward Linden Photography

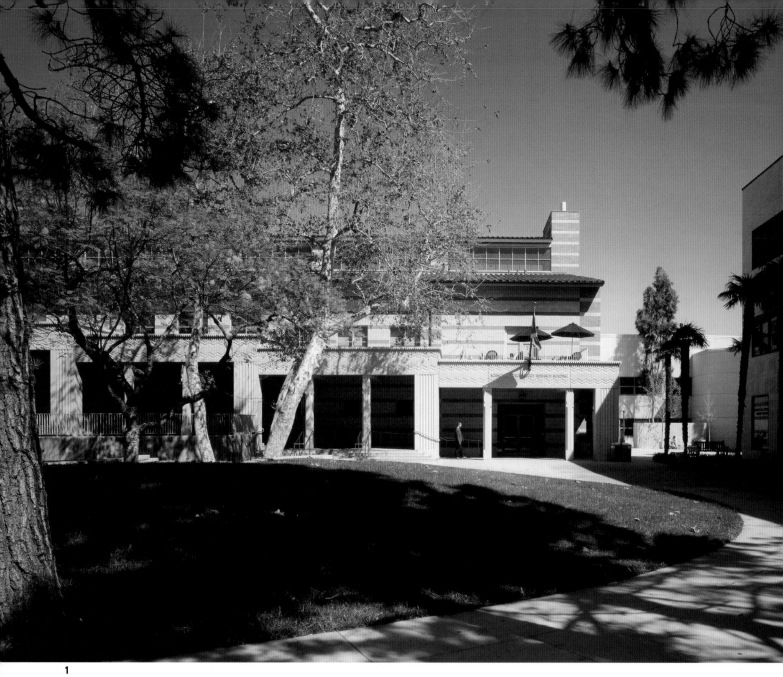

1

2

The Science and Technology Research Building is a physics and engineering research facility, located at the southwest corner of the University of California's Los Angeles campus. The two-story facility comprises approximately 50,000 square feet of open high-bay and standard research space for the construction and running of large-scale experiments, concrete-shielded basement laboratory space, research support space, computer and electronics space, and a pedestrian arcade. The project also includes a service yard, landscaping and hardscape, existing site utilities relocations, remote utility points of connection, and modifications to the adjacent steam plant.

The exterior of the new building is a good fit with nearby buildings on this part of UCLA's campus. The building climbs a gentle slope, opening itself to a landscaped area via a concrete arcade and completing the third side of a quadrangle. The arcade is distinguished in its modern-revival style, complete with art-deco inspired surface reliefs. On top of the colonnade is a welcoming terrace with views out over the small quad. Because this building is basically a shed, the exterior wrapper becomes an opportunity for surface decoration that responds to the Southern California context. Brick and limestone banding encircles the building, breaking down its large scale and mediating the facility's long, flat walls.

Clerestory windows in a monitor that runs the length of the building flood the barn-like interior space with natural light. A glass wall within the space, dividing it longitudinally, allows natural light to fully penetrate the interior.

1   Building as it faces the landscaped quadrangle, with its articulated concrete arcade

2   The building's narrow end reveals its patterned brick façade

SCIENCE AND TECHNOLOGY RESEARCH BUILDING

University of California

AC Martin Partners

3   Basement space is utilitarian and devoted to heavy equipment
4   Overview of barn-like space, with light from roof monitor
5   Interior supports research work with large-scale equipment
Photography: John Edward Linden and Wolfgang Simon

4

5

1

2

SCIENCE CENTER

Designed expressly for contemporary teaching methods, this new Science Center enables Oberlin College in Oberlin, Ohio, to retain its national position as a premier educator of future scientists and also allows the departments of biology, chemistry, neuroscience, and physics, and a vastly enlarged science library, to be housed in one central location on campus.

Oberlin's existing science facility, the 1960s Kettering Science Building, created a 330-foot-long barrier (known on campus as 'The Great Wall of Science') along a heavily traveled roadway and pedestrian route (West Lorain), essentially cutting off the rest of the campus. This separation of the sciences from the surrounding campus created both a physical and intellectual schism. The design team took to heart Oberlin's programmatic, space, and image problems and created a science center as part of 150,000 square feet of new construction and 80,000 square feet of renovation.

The focus for both the client and the architects was to repair the existing science department fragmentation, support a more holistic approach linking diverse science disciplines, and create a stronger image for the sciences on campus. This project is unique in that the new building establishes a strong science presence in a primarily arts-based community, and extends the primary academic quad to include all the sciences. Located at the heart of Oberlin's residential and academic quad (with classical Cass Gilbert college buildings nearby), the new facility reinforces dominant campus use patterns by extending existing pathways through and around the campus with little interruption.

In keeping with modern pedagogical methods, the center's architecture blurs the distinction between the disciplines, allowing for growth and large-scale flexibility, while also melding some of Oberlin's campus landmarks into its design. Existing structures of different eras are integrated into the new science center. Internally, disciplines are arranged from left to right in a 'wave' of interdisciplinary adjacencies that share related utility infrastructures. These blurred boundaries allow for the growth of one department into another, and flexibility for spontaneous collaboration across specialties.

OBERLIN COLLEGE

PAYETTE ASSOCIATES

127

3

4

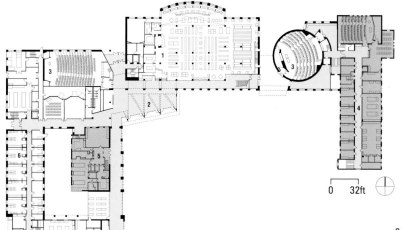

5

3 Pass-through to quad between the chemistry/science library and the physics building

4 Exterior detail of the commons area, as it looks out over the quad

5 Floor plan

6 Detail of skylights in commons area

7 Natural light dominates many interior spaces

6

7

Opposite:
 Interior of commons area, which is a bright welcoming space

9 Corridor from commons area, with library to left

Photography: Jeff Goldberg/Esto

1

2

As the first of its kind in the U.S., the $10-million Contained Research Facility's unique ability to provide natural research conditions in a highly secure, biologically contained environment will attract a wide range of users, including private biotechnology firms, federal and state agencies, and university research programs.

Located in the future agricultural enterprise zone of the University of California's Davis West Campus, the main building of the 24,000 square-foot complex provides modular Bio-Safety Level (BSL) 2 and 3 labs, growth chambers, greenhouses, and materials processing, each equipped with flexible services distribution systems designed for future adaptability. Other structures include an attached administrative building for reception, offices, and meeting rooms, and separate energy center housing major mechanical and electrical equipment.

In form, the exterior of the building has a domestic scale, with abstracted door and window elements, and a gable roof with chimneys. This simple use of materials contrasts with the greenhouse structure attached to its south side. A black canopy reaches out toward the parking area to welcome visitors. The gable roof space conceals the wealth of the building's mechanical equipment needed to provide the BSL-rated laboratories. The upper part of the building's volume is devoted to air-handling equipment that serves the labs on the first floor.

Interior spaces are treated in a straightforward manner, with the accent on utility and flexibility. Colors reflecting the exterior of the building are used throughout the interior, keeping the color palette simple and spare.

1   Overview of building from parking lot emphasizes its domestic scale

2   View of the building's welcoming entry, with sheltering canopy

CONTAINED RESEARCH FACILITY

UNIVERSITY OF CALIFORNIA

ANSHEN+ALLEN

133

3

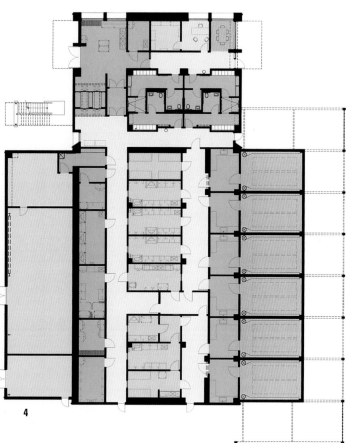

4

3 Greenhouse is used in conjunction with BSL-rated labs

4 Floor plan

5 Lab spaces painted dark color to suggest building's overall esthetic

6 View of mechanical equipment in concealed penthouse level of building

7 Lab spaces with a utilitarian feel

8 View from greenhouse corridor to ante room and greenhouse beyond

Photography: Robert Canfield Photography

5

6

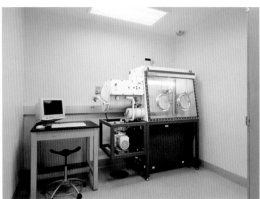

7

8

1

2

Two existing buildings are joined with new construction in this project to form a contemporary, multidisciplinary science center for Bowdoin College. Bowdoin's New Brunswick, Maine, campus is anchored by a central quadrangle framed by buildings representing a mosaic of architectural styles from several centuries. Each new addition to the campus expresses its own time while reinforcing this historic core.

Druckenmiller Hall is attached directly to Cleaveland Hall on one side and, by means of a third-level bridge, to Hatch Science Library on the other. The building has been strategically sited and designed to enhance the existing quadrangle while providing a new identity for the eastern edge of the campus and a more welcoming gesture to the Brunswick community. Corner entrances tie the new building to both the quad and the surrounding neighborhood.

The new facility contains classrooms, teaching and research laboratories, faculty offices, and conference rooms—all grouped around a central sky-lit atrium at the intersection of the new and the existing building components. This 'Commons' unifies circulation and provides opportunities for students and faculty to meet informally. On the second and third levels, also grouped around the atrium, are faculty offices, conference rooms, and teaching and research laboratories. The classrooms and laboratories offer exceptional flexibility, featuring modular layouts and movable walls.

Druckenmiller Hall's exterior harmonizes with the red brick of neighboring buildings while offering a design statement emblematic of the innovative teaching and research the complex supports. Glass and metal corners differentiate entrances, lounges, offices, and conference rooms from the laboratories and classrooms. This use of glass as a transitional material maintains the integrity of the connecting buildings and marks the corners of the new building. It also animates the façades and moderates the building mass, keeping the complex in harmony with the overall scale of the campus. During the day, these corners mirror the surrounding pine trees; at night they become welcoming beacons for students and town residents.

1   Glass corners illuminate the building as a welcoming beacon

2   Maintaining the rhythm of transparent corners, the triangular form of the greenhouse tops faculty offices and science center's receiving area

DRUCKENMILLER HALL OF SCIENCE

BOWDOIN COLLEGE

ELLENZWEIG ASSOCIATES

3 Exploded axonometric

4 Transparent connecting bridge and corner entrance reduces building's apparent scale while maintaining integrity of attached original chemistry building

5 Gray, perforated metal and stained maple stair provides an interior link and functions as a sculptural element in atrium

6 Campus entry opens into a two-story lobby where students and faculty mingle informally

7 Two-story central skylit atrium forms core of the complex, linking new and pre-existing buildings and creating a readily accessible gathering place for all disciplines

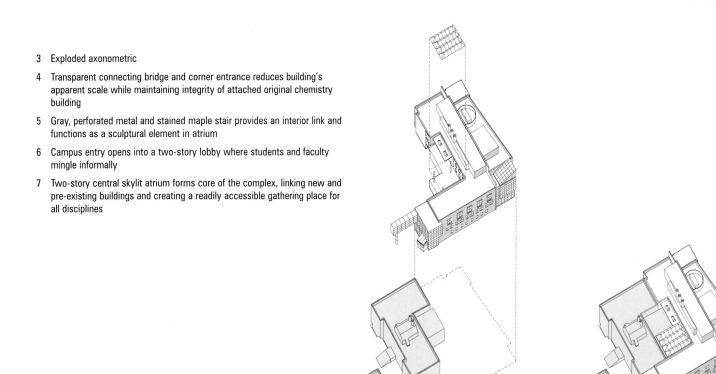

3

4

5

6

7

9

Opposite:
  Greenhouse occupies one full corner of the building's top floor, overlooking
  a grove of pine trees

9 Flexible teaching laboratory is designed to be used for either biology or
   chemistry instruction

10 A contemporary teaching laboratory for the college's biology department
    affords generous workspace

Photography: Steve Rosenthal

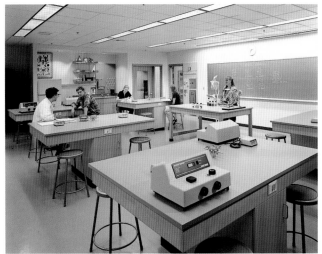

10

1

2

This new 208,000-square-foot, five-story building is the first of several buildings for the University of Connecticut's new 'Technology Quad,' which centralizes the science and engineering programs on its Storrs, Connecticut, campus.

The university's requests were that the building should serve as a gateway to the new quad, and that it should combine modern and traditional architectural forms with gable roofs. Thus, the architecture shows the influence of a number of buildings in and around the campus—the Collegiate Gothic central campus, old New England mills, and adjacent modern laboratories.

The Chemistry Building incorporates nine graduate and undergraduate divisions along with research labs for 30 professors and 150 graduate and postgraduate students. The building has separate wings for administration, teaching and research laboratories, and lecture halls. These simple rectangular wings are linked by a dramatic and complex four-story atrium space.

Materials and finishes are inspired by themes found in the discipline of chemistry. For example, bricks have been laid in merging bands of red and flashed-gray with the gray bands nearest the eaves on the main body of the building. Just below the eaves, the gray bricks turn into glazed black brick. This blending and darkening diminish the apparent height of the large building as well as make it appear less institutional, a request of the client. At key locations such as the main entry, and at rear façades surrounding the entry there, the bands arch or break into patterns of measurement. Inside, railings and floors have similar patterns. Likewise, the ceiling of the large auditorium 'morphs' from one wave to another, front to rear. All this mixing and measuring celebrates the spirit of chemistry.

1 Entry reaches out to passing students and faculty

2 View of chemistry building as it faces the pond

CHEMISTRY BUILDING

UNIVERSITY OF CONNECTICUT

CENTERBROOK ARCHITECTS

143

3

3   First floor allows students to take advantage of social spaces

4   Open atrium encourages views throughout building

5   Floor plan

6   Chemistry compound models in lab space

7   Fully outfitted typical laboratory space

Photography: Norman McGrath

4

5

1   Classroom
2   Computer lab
3   Instructional lab (undergraduate)
4   Sample/demo prep
5   Lecture hall
6   Outreach lab
7   Research lab
8   Stockroom/storage/workshop
9   Loading dock
10 Mechanical
11 Administrative offices
12 Faculty office
13 Atrium/lobby
14 Reading room/lounge

TEACHING

ADMINISTRATION/
FACULTY

RESEARCH

LECTURE HALL

13

SROOM   8 STOCK ROOM/STORAGE/

0   40ft

6

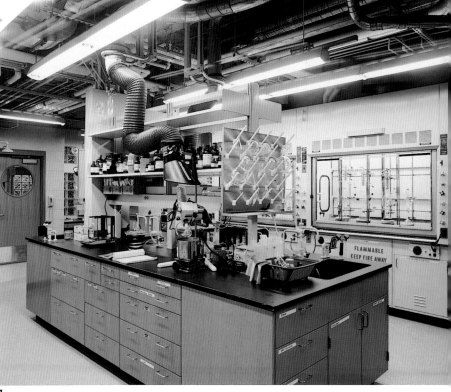

7

The ambition of this project was to bring a physical vitality and a new sense of community to the College of Engineering on the Iowa City campus. The existing building, constructed as a series of additions over many years, was internally fragmented without any unifying public or social space. The exterior was uniform in its classical expression, but lacked a major public entrance and a sense of openness appropriate to the college's mission. The addition opens the building to the campus mall to the south, with the main entrance and a new public face fronting a landscaped plaza. The internal fragmentation is remedied by reorganizing the circulation and adding public spaces to unite the new and existing spaces.

The 103,000-square-foot addition houses research and teaching laboratories, classrooms, seminar rooms and computer facilities. Two program elements—the student learning center and the student commons—form the project's public nucleus, around which the addition is organized. The 58,000-square-foot renovation improves and modernizes existing spaces including the library and faculty offices, and updates the building's mechanical and electrical systems.

The student commons gives the college a new social focal point. The adjacent atrium with its continuous skylight joins the addition to the south end of the existing building and brings natural light down through five levels. The learning center is an extension of the renovated library and is located in a skylit, double-height room on the second and third floors. Created by removing part of an existing wing, this open area brings light into the center of the complex, acts as a focal point for the north end of the building, and represents the academic core of the college. In contrast to both the library and the laboratory environments, the learning center is dedicated to team work areas and is envisioned as a hub for project-related student interchange.

Opposite:
Detail of metal façade, which reflects color of surrounding light and landscape

SEAMANS CENTER

UNIVERSITY OF IOWA

ANSHEN+ALLEN LOS ANGELES
(DESIGN ARCHITECT)
NEUMANN MONSON PC ARCHITECTS
(EXECUTIVE ARCHITECT)

2

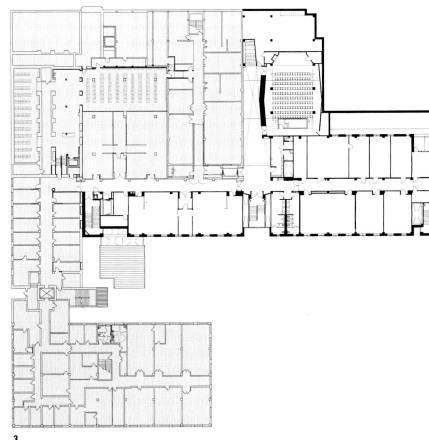

3

4

5

2 Building's form creates a welcoming forecourt

3 Floor plan

4 Courtyard offers places to sit and relax without leaving the building

5 Glazed element links new and old building

6 Atrium delivers natural light throughout building's interior

7   Lab spaces have high ceilings with exposed mechanical systems

8   Natural light floods lounge and study spaces

9   Warm wood finishes are used with elegant detailing

10 Ample illumination distinguishes lab spaces

Photography: Assassi Productions

8

9

10

1

2

3

4

5

6

This is one of the first research laboratories in the world designed to collect the majority of its own energy and water and recycle its waste. The laboratory was designed to consume close to 'net zero' energy and water.

The Smithsonian Tropical Research Institute in Bocas del Toro, Panama, is a leading center for basic research on the evolution, behavior, and ecology of tropical organisms. The site of the laboratory is a sensitive coastal area next to a mangrove swamp, on an island off Panama's Caribbean coast. The driving goal was to create a laboratory that minimizes its environmental impact without sacrificing its function as a scientific facility. To achieve this goal, the architects worked closely with the Smithsonian Institution's Melinda Humphrey Becker and Arup Engineers (International Builders was the contractor).

The building's main functions—labs for visiting and resident scientists, teaching spaces, conference facilities, and support spaces—occupy a string of volumes of approximately 5000 square feet (there are approximately 5000 square feet of outdoor work space and walkways). The interior spaces can be individually air-conditioned but the narrow, linear plan with a double roof also allows for natural cross ventilation, ample day-lighting, and passive solar shading. Raising the entire building on concrete piers not only helps to catch prevailing breezes for cooling, but also provides a measure of flood protection and minimizes the lab's impact on the site.

The upper roof consists of a 38 kW array of photovoltaic panels, interspersed with clear glass to allow light into the translucent lower roof, illuminating the interior spaces. The angled roof form directs rainwater to collection tanks at a central point on the building's lower level (to be completed at a later date). The filtered rainwater will then be used as the primary water supply, with backup provided by municipal water. Waste will be treated onsite with a constructed wetland, and the building's structure and wood finishes are of sustainable local hardwoods.

1   View of underside of permeable roof from west end
2   View of building from southeast
3   Translucent fiberglass ceiling visible in corridor accentuates natural lighting
4   From northeast, building appears as an extrusion
5   Lab work area with translucent fiberglass ceiling above
6   Warm native woods are used on exterior

Photography: Courtesy Kiss + Cathcart, Architects

BOCAS DEL TORO LABORATORY

KISS + CATHCART, ARCHITECTS

1

2

The Medical Education and Biomedical Research Facility (MEBRF) is the first phase of a masterplan for the health sciences campus at the University of Iowa. The far-reaching goal of the plan is to establish an academic campus in Iowa City, Iowa for the pursuit of excellence in education and research. Education is envisioned as the cohesive activity on the new campus, one that brings all the health sciences schools and colleges together along a main east–west pedestrian axis.

The new facility houses two programs. First, it functions as the new flagship for the university's Carver College of Medicine and is home to most of its educational, student, and administration spaces. Second, MEBRF provides state-of-the-art lab space for biomedical research. All the building's users come together in a communal four-story atrium, which includes a café and a 250-seat auditorium.

The atrium at the building's south is at the confluence of two major campus pathways and several other health sciences buildings. It is now the social and academic center on campus, accommodating the major pathway to the hospital, and is complemented by an open stair along the same axis. The auditorium is articulated as a large copper volume, providing a backdrop for the café and the lower atrium.

The design team was fortunate to work with the College of Medicine as a new medical curriculum was designed. The resulting spaces provide an environment matched to the needs of medical education. For example, the cluster of four 'student communities' takes the form of two-story spaces facing the central corridor on the west side and the quadrangle to the east. Each cluster includes open and private study space, social area, a classroom, and student support offices to provide the academic and social infrastructure of student life.

The repetitive and disciplined lab modules with identical windows on the upper floors are clad in local limestone. In contrast, spaces for the medical education program on the lower floors possess a sculptural variety, and are clad in weathered copper panels.

1   View of the complex from southeast, with atrium and gathering spaces at center

2   Building's curved façade reaches out to welcome visitors

MEDICAL EDUCATION AND BIOMEDICAL RESEARCH FACILITY

University of Iowa

Payette Associates

4

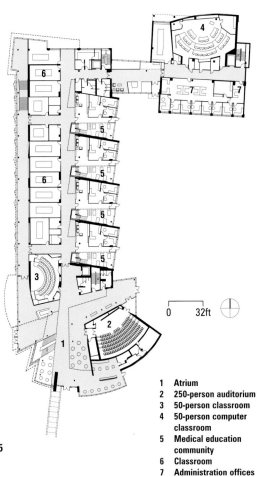

5

1 Atrium
2 250-person auditorium
3 50-person classroom
4 50-person computer classroom
5 Medical education community
6 Classroom
7 Administration offices

3 Central atrium is the crossroads of students and researchers

4 View of double-decker medical education spaces

5 Floor plan

6 Labs' glass walls maximize light and views

7 Medical education classrooms are encased in glass walls

Photography: Jeff Golderg/Esto

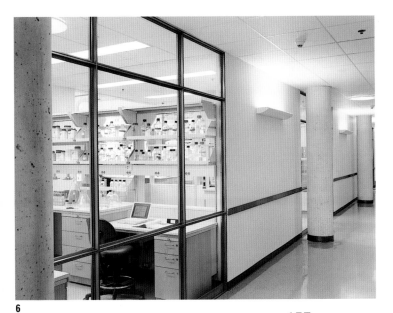

6

7

The Naito Chemistry and Bauer Laboratory Building and Center for Genomics Research unifies three formerly disconnected buildings, completing the quadrangle of Harvard University's Cabot Science Complex in Cambridge, Massachusetts. The entire courtyard was built atop an expansive 40,000-square-foot basement, linking Naito and Bauer underground to all the surrounding buildings of the complex. Connections between facilities have also been enhanced through the extensive new pedestrian landscape, and by a three-story glass bridge to the Sherman-Fairchild Biochemistry Laboratory.

The Naito and Bauer Building accommodates two fundamentally different laboratory types, unified by a single architectural expression. In Naito Chemistry, more traditional laboratories are built around large research groups, led by individual principal investigators in Physical Chemistry, Chemical Biology, and Organic Chemistry. Conversely, the Bauer Laboratory was not designed for permanent faculty. Rather, it brings together research fellows from varying scientific disciplines by providing state-of-the-art, flexible, completely transparent labs for Genomics, Proteomics, and Bioinformatics. Defined by its research mission and reinforced by this location on campus, the Naito and Bauer Building was conceived as connective tissue. It stands at the intersection of Harvard's Departments of Chemistry and Biology.

The key challenge for the building exterior was the reconciliation of a contemporary architectural expression with the more traditional language of its immediate neighbors. The combination of terracotta-colored sandstone panels and articulated glass curtain walls provide a modern, optimistic variation to the prevalent red brick and limestone vernacular in this section of campus. The curtain wall permits abundant amounts of natural light to the laboratories and offices within.

The new pedestrian environment created by the redesign of Cabot Courtyard and Frisbie Place not only unites the buildings of the Cabot Science Complex, but also integrates this area with the surrounding campus. The landscape's geometric patches of lawn, long black granite benches, and café tables with parasol tops all create opportunities for casual interaction and relaxation outside of the laboratory.

Opposite:
Naito and Bauer Building's terra cotta-colored sandstone continues the red-brick coloration of its neighbors, while abundant curtain wall conveys a more contemporary expression

NAITO CHEMISTRY AND BAUER LABORATORY BUILDING AND CENTER FOR GENOMICS RESEARCH

HARVARD UNIVERSITY

ELLENZWEIG ASSOCIATES

2

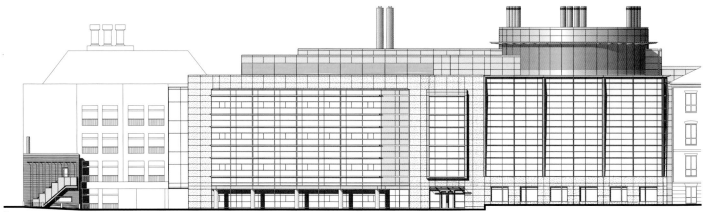

3

4

5

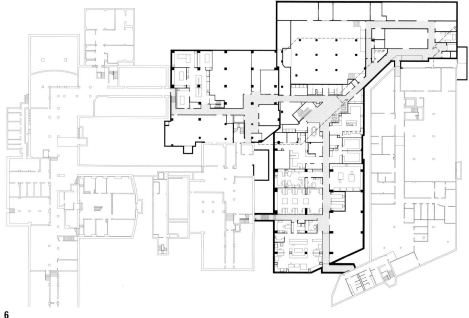

6

2   Reflections of the Peabody Museum and
    Mallinckrodt Laboratory animate the glass façades
    of the Naito and Bauer Building; a curved brick
    path connects pedestrians to the main entrance
    from Frisbie Place

3   Elevation

4   Hierarchy of pedestrian paths across Cabot
    Courtyard in abstract patterns of brick, concrete,
    and grass.

5   Dynamic portal between Cabot Courtyard and
    Frisbie Place beyond

6   Floor plan

7

8

7 Layers of space in the Bauer Laboratory, are all visible through a series of glass walls

8 Cradled by an acoustical maple wall and ceiling, soft seating in the lobby provides a quiet spot for contemplating the gallery's high-resolution photographs of past research projects

9 The building's expansive north curtain wall recruits the façade of the nearby Peabody Museum as the 'fourth wall' of an upper floor organic chemistry lab in Naito Chemistry

10 High-definition plasma screens in the lobby's cyber-café broadcast kinetic images of ongoing research projects

11 In Naito Chemistry, custom-designed, stainless steel fume hoods provide ample space for large experiments

12 In a Naito chemistry break room, researchers can monitor activities in either the physical chemistry laboratory or the write-up area beyond

Photography: Anton Grassl (7,12), Edward Jacoby (8,10), Steve Rosenthal (9,11), Sam Gray Photography (p.158, 2,4,5,6)

9

10

11

12

1

2

The adaptive reuse of the 380,000-square-foot Franklin Wilkins Building (built in the early 1900s as a warehouse) provides modern research and teaching facilities for the college's London campus into the new millennium.

The design of the exterior focuses on pedestrian interaction with the building. New, grandly scaled entrances carved into the existing warehouse façade are designed to increase the level of transparency from the street of the main interior space. Additionally, new display windows and storefront windows line the street level. Contrasting the existing building is the insertion of new aluminum panel cladding and glazed entries.

Redefining the first floor rather than the existing ground floor as the main level increases the floor area near the entries. This also allows for an 'event floor' that can be viewed from inside an out.

The main public space for the building is the Great Hall, which acts as the main quad for what is essentially a campus within a building. It is designed to be an active, animated place with circulation routed both horizontally and vertically. The Great Hall is activated by the adjacent functions of a two-story social/dining space, an overlooking two-story library, and a cross-axial stacked classroom corridor. The experience is crowned by a restored skylight that runs parallel to the angle that threads its way through the space.

To counteract the limitations of the existing low ceilings, visual access to vertical spaces is exploited and each of three existing light wells becomes the center of a key public zone. The central light well over the Great Hall is the heart of the building. The west light well connects the two floors of social/dining space and provides outdoor access. The east light well becomes a double-height study room/computer lab for the library. Thus, the light wells of old are transformed into the key celebratory elements for this new facility.

1   New entry has accent on transparency and views into the building

2   Converted building still has bearing of early 1900s warehouse

FRANKLIN WILKINS BUILDING

KING'S COLLEGE

ANSHEN+ALLEN

3

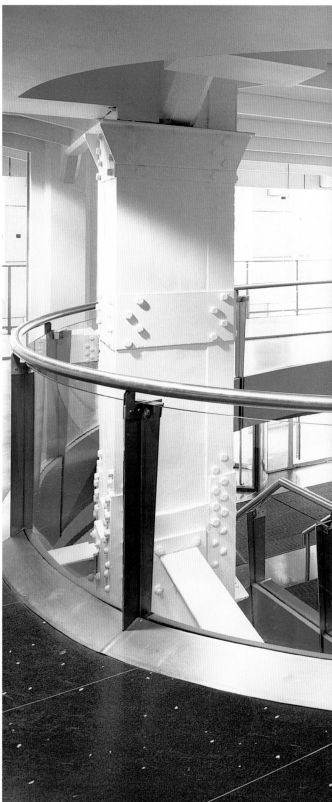

5

4

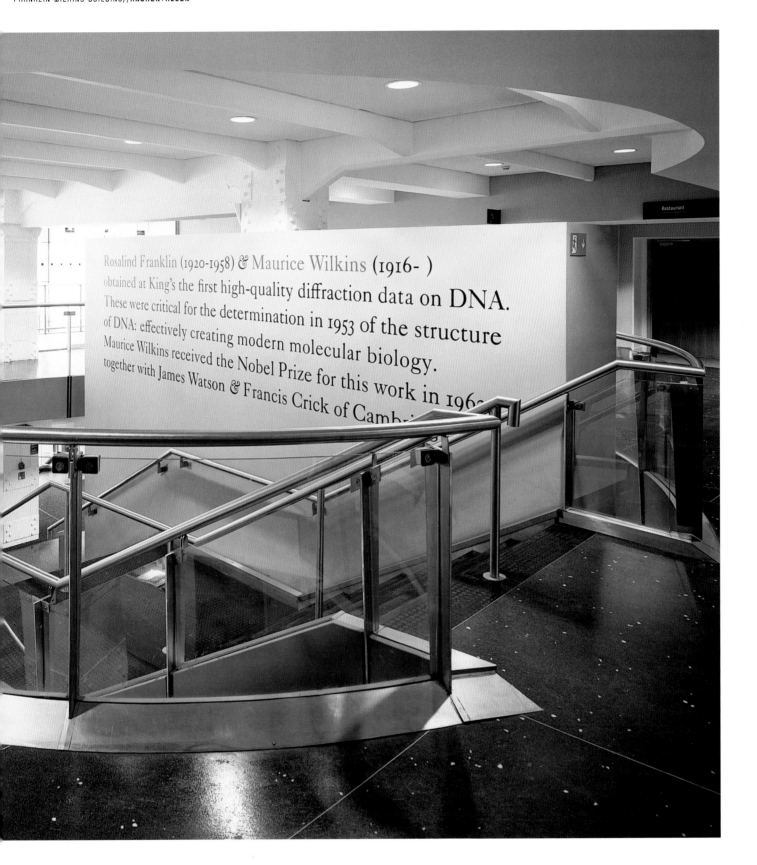

Rosalind Franklin (1920-1958) & Maurice Wilkins (1916-) obtained at King's the first high-quality diffraction data on DNA. These were critical for the determination in 1953 of the structure of DNA: effectively creating modern molecular biology. Maurice Wilkins received the Nobel Prize for this work in 1962 together with James Watson & Francis Crick of Cambridge.

3 New social/dining space is overlooked by library

4 View of well-lit library space

5 New central stair is in contrast to existing architectural context

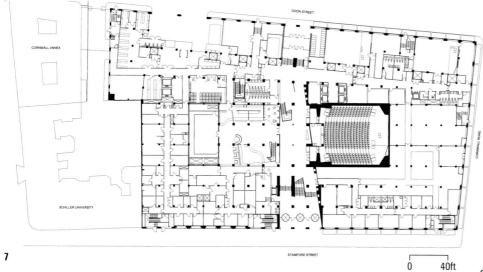

7

Opposite:
Staircase under atrium's natural light

7 Floor plan

8 Auditorium uses light woods and dark furnishings for contrast

Photography: John Edward Linden Photography

8

1

2

The Learning Laboratory for Complex Systems at MIT in Cambridge, Massachusetts, is a unique combination of integrated teaching laboratories modeled after real-world technological and engineering processes. Applying lessons of the workplace to the academic setting, the new program works as a collaborative, physical environment supporting strategic mission, productivity, and recruitment.

Combining classroom functions and hands-on environments, the Learning Laboratory physically translates the pedagogical approach of MIT's Department of Aeronautics and Astronautics—to encompass the full range of engineering process skills in Conceive, Design, Implement and Operate (CDIO) complex systems, beyond the traditional disciplines of analysis and design.

The historic Daniel Guggenheim Aeronautical Laboratory was renovated and expanded as a highly flexible, open space that allows students and faculty to work in team environments on projects of varying size and complexity. The design reorganizes the 50,000-square-foot building and its maze of corridors to promote communication between different teaching, research, and lab activities, as well as between students and faculty. The building is zoned functionally, with conceptual work taking place on the upper floors, design occurring on the second and third floors, implementation on the main floor labs, and operations testing on the lower floor labs and shops and in the new student space known as the 'hangar.' All of these uses, the library, and student resources are visible and accessible from the central space and the new interconnecting stair, creating visual and physical openness.

Labs combine computer simulation with hands-on testing in open, flexible space. The lower level is open to natural light. It is directly accessible to students from the main labs or from the 'dirty' lab spaces with testing equipment and power tools. Flexible partitions and hanging and projection surfaces define project space and provide overhead access to power and data. The 6000-square-foot, three-story hangar supports work on unusually large aerospace assignments and student-run independent projects, and adds new connections to all three main student levels.

1   New 'hangar' with design loft and over-sized project space
2   Restored exterior of historic Guggenheim Laboratory/Building 33

LEARNING LABORATORY FOR COMPLEX SYSTEMS

MASSACHUSETTS INSTITUTE OF TECHNOLOGY

CAMBRIDGE SEVEN ASSOCIATES, INC.

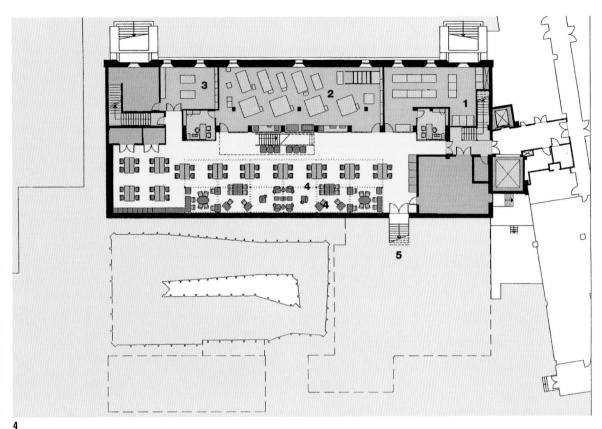

1   Instrumentation laboratory
2   Machine shop
3   Composite shop
4   Small project implementation
    and operation
5   Hangar and wind tunnel
    operations above

4

5

Opposite:
Flexible teaching space, with library beyond

4   Floor plan

5   View of Gelb labs below

6

7

8

6   View across stairs connecting Seamans to Gelb labs below

7   View of library, now integrated into the teaching space

8   Gelb labs with machine show and 'hangar' beyond

9   Operations center in the new 'hangar' addition

Photography: Nick Wheeler

9

1

2

erstacker Science Hall at Hiram College is a 31,230-square-foot science facility that consists of flexible teaching and research space for biology and chemistry.

Gerstacker Science Hall at Hiram College is a 31,230-square-foot science facility that consists of flexible teaching and research space for biology and chemistry.

The building form takes its cues from the Georgian architecture of the college's Hiram, Ohio, campus. Providing a common space where students and faculty from the biology and chemistry departments can interact, a major public space is located above the new campus entrance gate created by the building, linking departments both symbolically and literally. Above and to either side of this room, traditional roof forms are manipulated to allow the venting of fume hood exhaust through a series of appropriately scaled chimneys. This attitude was carried throughout the building, allowing for the seamless integration of robust mechanical systems into traditional architectural forms.

Laboratories were designed with primary utilities at the perimeter, and movable tables inboard. This arrangement allows the conversion of the room from project-based work to a lecture setting in a matter of minutes. In cases where it was not appropriate to move laboratory equipment, the need for flexibility was addressed by the creation of a number of work venues in a single lab suite. Thus, flexible lab/lecture areas were supplemented by the provision of immediately adjacent wet labs. Similarly, in the organic chemistry labs, fume hoods are grouped around a central shared work/meeting table, with dedicated equipment rooms located in an adjacent space. The design team worked closely with Hiram faculty to devise these arrangements, which promise to be readily adaptable to a wide variety of teaching/research needs.

1 Front façade of building responds to Georgian architecture of campus

2 Building entrance allows a pass-through from one part of campus to another

GERSTACKER SCIENCE HALL

HIRAM COLLEGE

BURT HILL KOSAR RITTELMANN ASSOCIATES

177

3

4

5

3 Overview of lab space with simple detailing

4 Built-in lab cabinets reduce clutter in the lab environment

5 Moving lab desks can easily transform space for lecture instruction

6 Floor plan

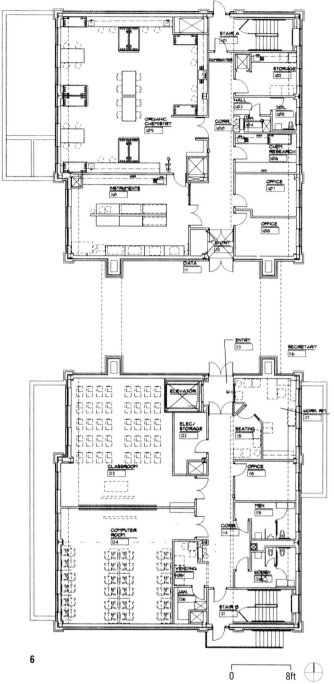

6

0   8ft

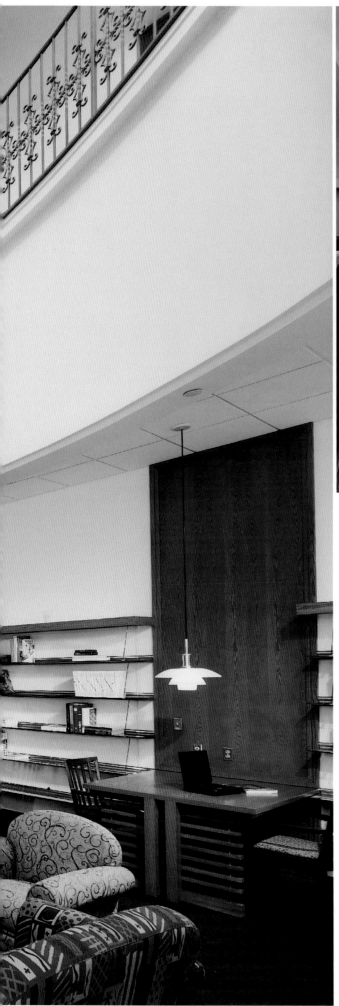

8

9

7   Lounge space with connecting spiral stair encourages collaboration

8   Double-height lounge space is sunny and inviting

9   Built-in desks are a feature of the interior

Photography: Edward Massery

1

2

3

The biochemistry/NMR facility on the University of Wisconsin's Madison campus accommodates the activities of this prominent department engaged in basic research in the biochemical sciences. Within 198,000 square feet of space, the building houses up to 288 researchers in 23 lab groups. The building also contains a 21,780-square-foot National Magnetic Resonance Facility, one of only two facilities of its size in the nation. Major goals for the project were to provide modern laboratory space for a diversity of existing research programs and to facilitate future recruiting of faculty and students.

The building is organized around two atriums and associated open stairways, which bring natural light deep into the building and provide a sense of connection from one floor to the next. Around the atriums are a variety of areas that foster interaction, including lunchrooms, conference rooms, the library, the elevators, and informal gathering places.

Office and laboratory areas are designed as retreats where the real work of the department can be carried out with few distractions. When researchers leave the offices and labs, their normal destinations are the interaction areas around the atriums, where they will encounter colleagues. A bridge connects the new building to the other biochemistry department research wings. The building also houses the departmental front office, plant growth chamber space, a 60-seat auditorium with a modern audiovisual system, and a dramatic space housing the National Magnetic Resonance Facility at Madison (NMRFAM).

The design reinterprets traditional forms and materials found on campus to create a new and intriguing building that is comfortably settled into the campus. Careful articulation of the façade through small panels of glass brings a comfortable sense of scale to the tall floor-to-floor heights required in a laboratory building.

Circulation and wayfinding within are made easy through the pair of atria and the resulting abundance of natural light. The work environment is uniquely suited to the researchers' needs, providing technology and comfort, privacy, and space for easy interaction.

BIOCHEMISTRY BUILDING/NMR FACILITY

UNIVERSITY OF WISCONSIN

FLAD ASSOCIATES

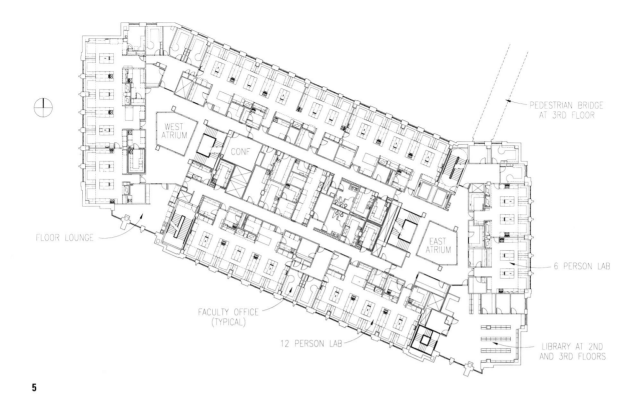

5

6

7

Opposite:
   Ample staircase with lounge areas encourages informal meetings and
   collaboration

5   Floor plan

6   Lobby floor design is a contrast to its restrained use of color

7   Lab areas display large exterior windows for light and views

Photography: Christopher Barrett/Hedrich-Blessing

185

The new Science Center on the college's Santa Monica, California campus helps knit together a haphazard collection of structures dating from the 1950s, with a clear modern building organized around quadrangles.

The 99,500-square-foot center replaces an earlier building that was severely damaged in the 1994 Northridge earthquake, and consists of a three-story laboratory building and a two-story classroom/faculty office building centered on a courtyard. New teaching labs are designed to accommodate the life sciences and physical sciences departments (physics, chemistry, biology, microbiology, anatomy, botany, marine biology and zoology). There is also a computer learning center and two large lecture halls.

The site is adjacent the college's original quadrangle. To preserve the quad's scale the program was split into two parallel buildings, offset from each other to create open squares. A two-story wing redefines the edge of the original quad while a four-story wing, located behind, marks the eastern edge of the campus.

The moderate climate allows the classroom/office building to use natural ventilation and shading. Wide breezeways cut through the classroom building and visually connect the science court and the main quadrangle. Individual classrooms are entered from either the science court or the quad through a series of glazed porches, with views to the gardens on either side. The classroom building is cooled by prevailing ocean breezes through a combination of operable windows and rooftop exhaust chimneys.

The Science Center's exterior is a layering of simple repetitive elements. Both buildings are plaster-clad volumes connected by a system of outdoor circulation balconies clad in metal panels that are demountable for access to the laboratory's piping systems. Stainless steel fabric stretched between steel tubes provides a vertical counterpoint to the façade's balconies, which in turn are supported by concrete columns running the length of the courtyard. Both buildings are set within gardens used by the Botany Department.

Opposite:
Example of the building's expressive structure

SCIENCE CENTER

SANTA MONICA COLLEGE

ANSHEN+ALLEN LOS ANGELES

Opposite:
Courtyard in the evening become a welcoming place to congregate

3   Interior court is a welcoming, protected space

4   First floor plan

5   Building's forms are simple yet powerful under the California sun

6   Sunshade mitigates glare into building and offers welcoming canopy

3

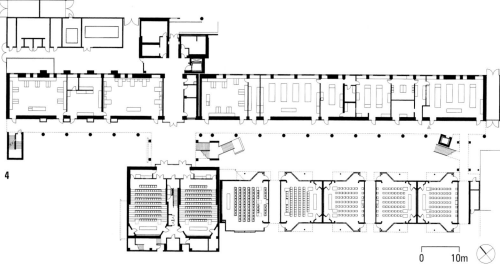

4

0   10m

5

6

7

7 Muscular steel framing in the greenhouse

8 Open framework allows for the display of science exhibits

9 Upper deck walkway offers some privacy through screening

10 Screen material is used to allow air movement while cutting sun

11 Typical lab and teaching space

12 Entry to center is marked by dramatic roof

Photography: Tom Bonner Photography

8

9

10

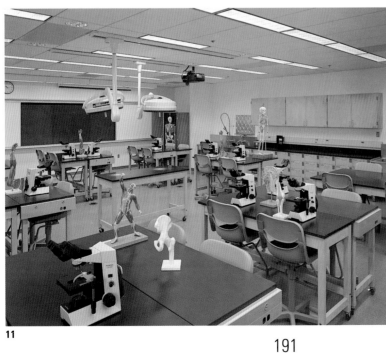

11

12

1

2

This well-known private prep school in Exeter, New Hampshire, uses a teaching method focused on the 'Harkness Table,' a 7-foot-by-11-foot oval table that seats 12 students and a teacher who present and discuss their work in a participatory format. The program for the new Phelps Science Center was to adapt the Harkness method of teaching to the science curriculum. The architects were asked to rethink typical educational laboratory design to accommodate this pedagogical approach. To test the workability and verify this unique design, a prototype classroom was built in the existing science building and tested by various classes for more than a year.

Chemistry, physics, biology, multi-science, and computer science constitute the subject areas taught at Phelps. The classrooms of each discipline surround a common lab where two or more classes can participate in experiments. Full-height glass partitions at common labs invite passersby to take a look at science as it unfolds.

The skylit atrium lobby contains the central stairs, a seawater aquarium, the skeleton of a humpback whale recovered by teachers and students from a beach in Maine, and a student lounge. Used as a gathering and exhibit space, as well as to accommodate specific physics experiments, the atrium's terrazzo floor pattern is an abstract representation of the midnight sky on the date of the building's dedication.

The building contains Grainger Auditorium, a multipurpose flat-floor room that can be divided into two separate spaces. The auditorium accommodates 250 to 300 people depending on the configuration of seating. Movable platforms supporting tables wired with power and data allow for teaching seminars.

The architectural character of the building fits comfortably in a handsome New England campus that has evolved over more than 200 years. The east façade holds the street line while it forms an outdoor classroom and wetland teaching garden surrounded by adjacent buildings to the south and west.

1   A landscaped entry court with seating frames building entrance
2   Physics lab with its curved glass wall

PHELPS SCIENCE CENTER

PHILLIPS EXETER ACADEMY

CENTERBROOK ARCHITECTS

193

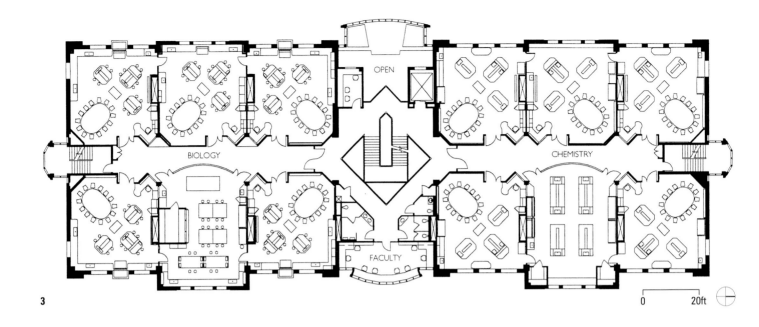

3

BIOLOGY   OPEN   CHEMISTRY

FACULTY

0   20ft

4

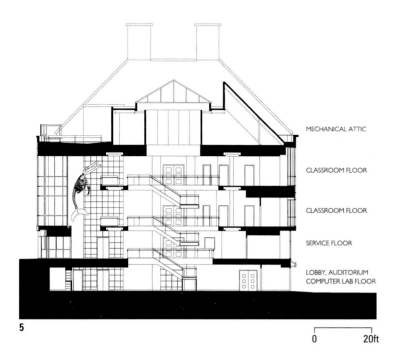

MECHANICAL ATTIC

CLASSROOM FLOOR

CLASSROOM FLOOR

SERVICE FLOOR

LOBBY, AUDITORIUM
COMPUTER LAB FLOOR

5

0   20ft

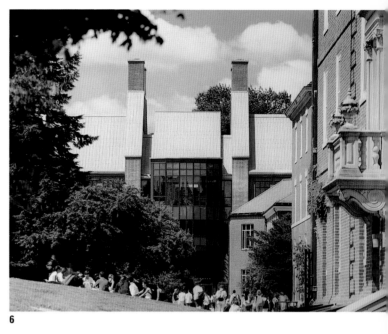

6

7

3   Second floor plan

4   View of multi-story lounge space with display of sea creatures

5   Building section

6   Building in the context of its traditional campus architecture

7   Lab spaces found just off central staircase

8   Central stair is a place of student energy and activity

Photography: Jeff Goldberg/Esto

195

8

1

2

The Genomics and Proteomics Research Building is devoted to cross-disciplinary research within the McGill University Health Centre. The site, on the slope of Mount Royal, is located in the science and technology precinct of McGill's Montreal campus.

As a metaphor for the scientific research process, the building embodies the concepts of experimentation, observation, and communication. The plan is organized by a central north–south corridor and service spine, and its section by stacked multi-story atria. The lower atrium, with its main entrance on the street, links the city to the campus. The laboratories are located on the east side of the building. Across the corridor on the west side are the bio-informatics offices, meeting rooms, and administrative spaces where the collected data is analyzed.

The upper atrium forms the heart of the new facility. This three-story space functions as a catalyst for interaction between the building's users—a place where ideas and knowledge are shared. The projecting teleconference room reads as the building's oculus, the metaphorical eye-piece of the scientific instrument, overlooking Rutherford Park/Reservoir, the mountain and city beyond. The atrium is an open vertical slot juxtaposed with the more shuttered nature of the west elevation.

The building's massing is tripartite, composed of a three-story glass 'research box' perched atop a solid limestone base, and capped with a metal-clad penthouse. On the west side of the building, a series of canted planes clad with diaphanous mesh scrims control the intense, low altitude afternoon sun.

The materials reinforce the idea of transparency. Glass, both inside and outside the building, is used for its ability to refract, reflect, distort, and transmit light and movement. As an extension of the glass concept, stainless steel mesh, on the exterior west-facing sunscreens and in the interior as scrims, filters and reflects light. The base of the building is constructed from reclaimed limestone from the original Donner medical research building. This green solution builds both metaphorically and physically on the foundations of scientific research at the site.

1 Building facing onto the main thoroughfare
2 Building facing west, with its transparent stainless steel screens

GENOMICS AND PROTEOMICS RESEARCH BUILDING

McGill University

Kuwabara, Payne McKenna Blumberg Architects

Fichten Soiferman and Associates, Architects

3

4

5

6

7

8

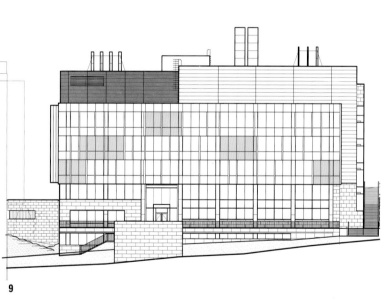

9

3   Detail of central stair with elevators beyond

4   View of the side stair that connects third and fourth levels

5   Typical lab space is open and light-filled

6   Central stair is a glass-enclosed object at building's center

7   Conference spaces and work areas have sliding glass walls

8   Detail of façade, which incorporates stainless steel mesh to filter light

9   Elevation

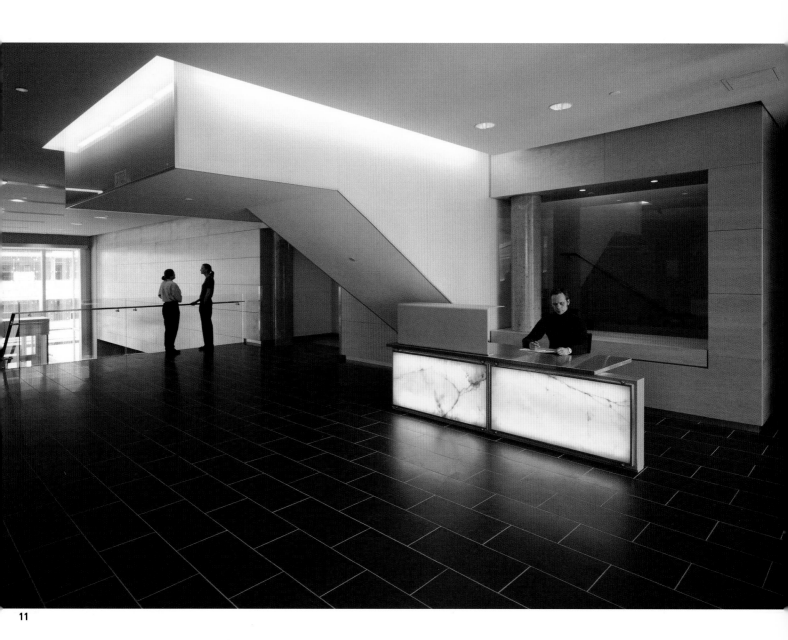

11

10   Central stair, the main method of circulation, shimmers with metal scrim
11   Reception space on the fourth level has an illuminated marble desk
Photography: Michel Brunelle

1

2

3

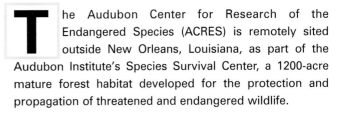

The Audubon Center for Research of the Endangered Species (ACRES) is remotely sited outside New Orleans, Louisiana, as part of the Audubon Institute's Species Survival Center, a 1200-acre mature forest habitat developed for the protection and propagation of threatened and endangered wildlife.

This 35,000-square-foot facility provides for laboratory research in reproductive biology and physiology, endocrinology, and genetics, and includes surgical suites for embryo transfer along with facilities in cryopreservation ('frozen zoo') to assure the future of endangered species through the banking of genetic materials. In addition to the research and medical labs, the center includes conference facilities for 100 people and administrative support services for the scientific staff of 40.

The client's mission—to connect people with nature by celebrating life through nature—is expressed architecturally in the relationship of the building to its context. The facility is sited deep with a clearing in the lowlands forest with entry across an extended boardwalk. The vertical and horizontal extension of masonry walls and floors through the building envelope blur the boundary between inside and outside. With the site, a captured outdoor space is created by the pinwheel organization of the plan. This more controlled space is set off from the rest of the scrub forest floor to provide a focused courtyard for the center. The pinwheel plan organization also provides a means to segregate the focused administrative and conference facilities.

The material qualities of the two construction systems (brick and wood) address the craft of construction and effectively merge the building with its natural context.

1 Building nestles into the natural surroundings

2 Entry court is a sunny, inviting space

3 Exterior materials blend light brick with dark-stained wood

AUDUBON CENTER FOR RESEARCH OF THE ENDANGERED SPECIES

ESKEW + DUMEZ + RIPPLE

4

5

6

4   Detail of corner expresses the building's materiality

5   Promenade to main entrance reaches out into the landscape

6   Building seamlessly blends indoor and outdoor spaces

7   Corridors admit ample light and render warmth of materials

8   Lab spaces have views out to the landscape

Photography: Timothy Hursley

7

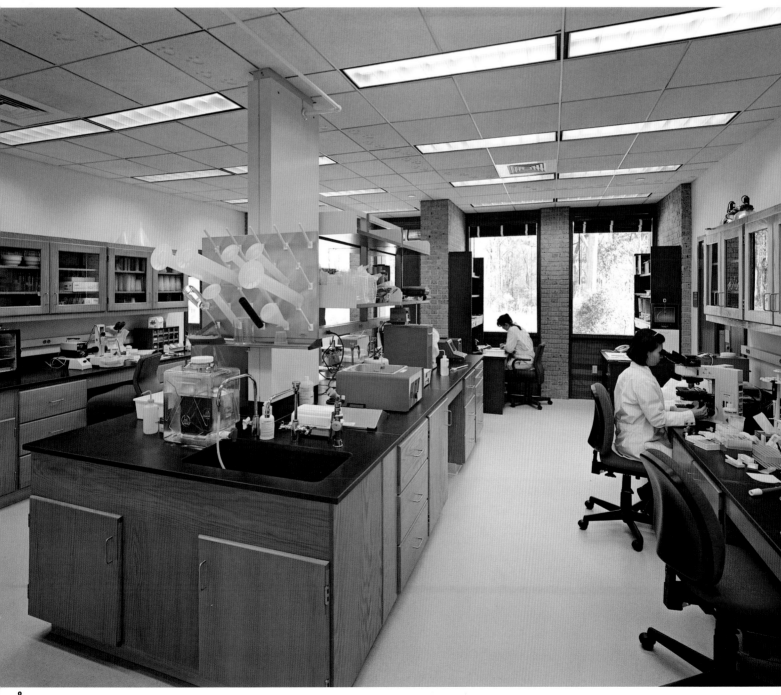

8

INDEX

Acknowledgments

Many people were involved in the creation of this book. Thanks are extended to the architects and designers who agreed to have their projects published and who supplied materials for this book, and to the private and public clients and institutions who commissioned them these path-breaking laboratories. Special gratitude is expressed to those photographers who generously allowed use of their photographs. The Introduction by Payette Associates, Inc., one of the most respected laboratory design architects in the world, is an invaluable addition to this book for which I am deeply grateful. Finally, thanks to Alessina Brooks and Paul Latham of The Images Publishing Group and its staff, especially Robyn Beaver, for their support of this publication, and for bringing it to fruition.

Author and Contributor Notes

Michael J. Crosbie is an internationally recognized author, architect, journalist, critic, and teacher. A former editor of both *Progressive Architecture* and *Architecture*, he is author of more than a dozen books on architecture. Dr Crosbie has written for a number of journals and magazines, including *Historic Preservation, Domus, Architectural Record, Landscape Architecture,* and *ArchitectureWeek*, and has won several journalism awards. He is currently the Editor-in-Chief of *Faith & Form* magazine. Dr Crosbie teaches architecture at Roger Williams University, and has lectured at architecture schools in North America and abroad. He practices with Steven Winter Associates, an architectural research and consulting firm in Norwalk, Connecticut.

Payette Associates, Inc., is a highly respected architecture firm that has been designing laboratories for more than a generation. Payette's lab buildings are found all over the world, and on many prestigious university campuses. The firm is based in Boston, Massachusetts.